Jüdisches Berlin
Jewish Life in Berlin

Bill Rebiger

Jüdisches Berlin
Jewish Life in Berlin

Photos aus Kaiserreich
und Weimarer Republik

Photos from the German Empire
and Weimar Republic

Jaron Verlag

Originalausgabe
1. Auflage 2008

www.jaron-verlag.de
Übersetzung: Miriamne Fields, Berlin
Umschlaggestaltung: Atelier Kattner, Berlin, unter Verwendung zweier Fotos aus dem Bildarchiv Preußischer Kulturbesitz
Layout: Prill Partners | producing, Berlin
Lithographie: LVD GmbH, Berlin
Druck und Bindung: Druckhaus Köthen GmbH

ISBN 978-3-89773-586-6

Jüdisches Leben in Berlin vor 1933

Jewish Life in Berlin before 1933

In unserer bildgesättigten Medienkultur einen Photoband zu veröffentlichen mag naiv, wenn nicht sogar überflüssig erscheinen. Heutzutage ertrinken wir in einer Bilderflut, die unentrinnbar über uns hinwegströmt. Selten gelingt es noch einem Bild, sich in uns festzusetzen, sich dem individuellen oder gar dem kulturellen Gedächtnis einzubrennen. Der abgeklärte Betrachter winkt ab: Alles schon gesehen!

Längst haben wir das Vertrauen in die Wahrheit und Unschuld der Bilder verloren. Wir wissen um die Manipulierbarkeit von Bildern und die Manipulierung durch Bilder. Durch die schier unbegrenzten Möglichkeiten digitaler Bildbearbeitung und die psychologische Raffinesse cleverer Werbestrategen können Bilder inhaltlich modifiziert und für jegliche Interessen instrumentalisiert werden. Aber auch die gute alte analoge Photographie, die noch mit Platte oder Film arbeitete, taugt nicht zwangsläufig als authentische Quelle für historische Fragestellungen. Nicht nur das Atelierphoto bildet Posen ab, sondern selbst jeder Schnappschuss stellt eine Inszenierung und Interpretation von Wirklichkeit dar. Der subjektive Blick des Photographen entscheidet letztlich, was photographiert wird und was nicht. Das bedeutet, dass wir eigentlich bei jedem Bild auch das berücksichtigen müssten, was jenseits des Bildrandes und der Belichtungszeit zu sehen war. (Von den unsichtbaren, das heißt nicht abbildbaren Wahrheiten soll an dieser Stelle erst gar nicht die Rede sein.) Zugleich liegt aber auch im subjektiven Blick des Betrachters alter Bilder die Gefahr, dass eine vermeintlich goldene Vergangenheit verklärt wird, dass eigene Wunsch- und Idealvorstellungen in das Bild projiziert und Klischees reproduziert werden.

Dieser Bildband unternimmt den Versuch, Photographien die Aufmerksamkeit zukommen zu lassen, die sie verdienen. Er versammelt nicht unüberschaubare Mengen kleinformatiger Bilder, sondern präsentiert eine begrenzte Anzahl

It may seem a bit naive, perhaps even a bit redundant, to publish a book of photos in this image-saturated media world that we live in today. We are constantly being exposed to a flood of pictures that inevitably slide right by us. Rarely does an image stick with us, engraving itself in our individual memory or cultural consciousness. The detached observer simply dismisses it. Seen it all before!

We lost our faith in the truth and innocence of pictures a long time ago. We all know now that pictures can be manipulated and used to manipulate us. The unlimited possibilities created by digital processing and the psychological sophistication of clever advertising make it possible to alter the content of a picture and exploit it for any desired purpose. But even good old-fashioned analogue photography with its use of plates and film is not necessarily accepted anymore as an authentic source for historical documentation. Posed pictures are not only made in a photo studio, every snapshot is a staged presentation and interpretation of the truth. The photographer, using his subjective view, ultimately determines what to photograph and what to leave out. This means that whenever we look at a picture, we should really be asking ourselves what existed beyond the picture frame and after the period of exposure ended. (Not to mention the unseeable or unpresentable truth which cannot be considered here.) There is always a risk that when older photographs are viewed subjectively, they will convey a distorted, romantic impression of a golden past. The observer projects his own desires and ideals onto the picture and consequently reproduces clichés.

This book of photographs is an attempt to give pictures the attention that they deserve. This is not a large collection of images in a small format. Instead it's a selection of a few informative photographs re-printed with quality and a size that allows for a high degree of detail to bring us into contact with pictures we can't

aussagefähiger Photographien in hochwertiger Reproduktionsqualität und detailreicher Bildgröße. So erreichen uns vielleicht Bilder, denen wir nicht entkommen, die uns verfolgen, vor denen wir uns nicht verschließen können. Manchmal blicken wir vielleicht in die Augen längst Verstorbener, die uns tief in die Seele schauen. Mitunter vermag ein Bild etwas auszudrücken, das kaum oder gar nicht in Worte zu fassen ist. Vielleicht beschwört ein Bild eine Vergangenheit herauf, die man vergessen glaubte oder die man nicht mehr für möglich hielt.

Wenn für den aufgeklärten Zeitgenossen eine Epoche wie ein Alpdruck unsere nationale Identität negativ bestimmt, dann die Zeit des Nationalsozialismus. Die Schoa, die Vernichtung des europäischen Judentums, stellt eine Zäsur dar, die unzureichend als Zivilisationsbruch bezeichnet wird. Das bedeutet aber nicht nur, dass der Blick auf die Zeit von 1933 bis 1945 und auch auf die Jahre danach von unserem Wissen um den nationalsozialistischen Schrecken geprägt ist, sondern es bedeutet auch, dass sogar die Betrachtung der Zeit vor 1933 unweigerlich auf dieses Fanal deutscher Geschichte gerichtet ist. Der Schriftsteller Günter Kunert nannte daher Bilder vom Judentum aus Kaiserzeit und Weimarer Republik treffenderweise Bilder aus einer deutschen Vor-Vergangenheit. Dieses Davor ist nicht mehr zu lösen von der nachfolgenden Vergangenheit, der Zeit des Nationalsozialismus. Die unauslöschlichen Bilder von mit Davidsternen beschmierten Schaufenstern am Boykott-Tag 1933, von brennenden Synagogen beim Novemberpogrom 1938, von gehetzten Juden mit aufgenähtem gelbem Stern ab 1941 und von Leichenbergen der Massenvernichtungs- und Konzentrationslager bis 1945 legen sich unweigerlich über die Bilder von Juden vor 1933. Je näher die Bilder diesem Jahr kommen, desto mehr fragt sich der Betrachter: Was ist aus den Menschen geworden, die wir auf diesen Bildern sehen? Konnten sie sich noch durch Emigration, Flucht oder Verstecken retten, oder wurden sie inhaftiert, deportiert und ermordet?

Die hier vorliegenden Photographien zeigen die Vielfalt jüdischen Lebens im Berlin der Kaiserzeit und der Weimarer Republik. Die gerne

ignore, pictures that will continue to haunt us, pictures we can't close ourselves off from. When we view some of these photos we find ourselves looking into the eyes of someone long deceased, and their glance seems to pierce our soul. Some of the pictures express something that can't be captured in words. A photo conjures up a past that we thought we had forgotten or didn't think was still possible.

National Socialism, more than any other period in history, has hauntingly affected our national identity in a negative way. The Shoah, the extermination of European Jewry, created a chasm that is often inadequately referred to as a break in civilization. This is an allusion to the fact that the period from 1933 to 1945 and the years that followed were deeply affected by the National Socialist tyranny. As a result, the period before 1933 was irrevocably overshadowed by this low point of German history. That's why author Günter Kunert aptly calls these pictures of Jews from the German Empire and Weimar Republic "pictures from a German pre-past." This "before" can no longer be separated from the period that followed, the period of National Socialism. The indelible images of store fronts smeared with the Star of David on the day of the 1933 boycott, photos of burning synagogues during the November pogrom of 1938, pictures of harassed Jews with a yellow star sewn onto their clothing after 1941, and finally, the heaps of corpses that piled up in the extermination and concentration camps until 1945 – these memories inevitably cast a shadow over the pictures of Jews who lived before 1933. As we look at the photos, and the year 1933 inches closer, we begin to ask ourselves the inevitable questions: What happened to the people we see here? Were they able to survive? Could they immigrate, flee or hide or were they arrested, deported and murdered?

The photographs presented here show the diversity of Jewish life in Berlin during the German Empire and Weimar Republic. The "heyday of German Judaism," as it is so often described, took place during this era. The Jews had finally succeeded in achieving equal rights as citizens of the Reich. But closer examination reveals that this "heyday" turned out to be nothing less than a chimera. Many Jewish people living during this

so genannte »Blütezeit des deutschen Judentums« fällt in diese Zeit. Immerhin war es endlich gelungen, die bürgerliche Gleichberechtigung der Juden gesetzlich zu garantieren. Aber diese »Blütezeit« entpuppt sich bei näherem Hinsehen als Schimäre. Zwar vollbrachten in dieser Zeit Menschen jüdischer Herkunft herausragende Leistungen auf den Gebieten der Wirtschaft, Wissenschaft und Kultur, aber zumeist als Deutsche unter Preisgabe ihrer jüdischen Identität. Die Abkehr vom Judentum kannte verschiedene Formen, so die Konversion zum Christentum, die Säkularisierung und das Vergessen der eigenen religiösen und kulturellen Tradition. Die verlogene Einseitigkeit einer solchen Assimilation war z.B. Gelehrten wie Gershom Scholem unerträglich.

Die Grenzen dieser Selbstaufgabe wurden schon sehr früh durch die Anfänge antisemitischer Aktivitäten aufgezeigt. Der Berliner Antisemitismusstreit um den Historiker Heinrich von Treitschke fiel bezeichnenderweise in die vielfach idealisierte Gründerzeit, ebenso die Gründung der »Antisemiten-Liga« durch Wilhelm Marr, die Gründung der antisemitischen »Christlich-Sozialen Arbeiterpartei« durch den evangelischen Hofprediger Adolf Stoecker oder die »Antisemiten-Petition« im Deutschen Reichstag. Diese verhängnisvolle Tradition wurde im Ersten Weltkrieg und vor allem in der Weimarer Republik fortgeführt und verstärkt. Die Ermordung des Außenministers Walther Rathenau 1922 und die antisemitischen Ausschreitungen im Berliner Scheunenviertel 1923 waren traurige Vorboten des nachfolgenden Nationalsozialismus.

Die Herausbildung verschiedener religiöser Strömungen wie Reformjudentum und Neo-Orthodoxie wurde in der Kaiserzeit verfestigt. Nachdem sich in den 1860er Jahren das liberale Judentum als Hauptströmung nicht nur des Berliner Judentums etabliert hatte, formierte sich auf der Gegenseite auch die Minderheit orthodoxer Juden. So wurde 1869 in Berlin die Separatgemeinde »Gesetzestreue jüdische Religionsgesellschaft Adass-Jisroel« gegründet. Die geistig-geistlichen Fundamente beider Strömungen des Judentums wurden jeweils wissenschaftlich in privaten Lehreinrichtungen gelegt, da es

time achieved great accomplishments in the field of economics, science and culture, but they did so as Germans, having abandoned their Jewish heritage. Jews turned away from their Jewish past in many different ways – through conversion to Christianity, through secularization or by disregarding the religious and cultural traditions they had grown up with. The misleading one-sidedness of this kind of assimilation was intolerable to scholars like Gershom Scholem.

The early emergence of anti-Semitic activities soon made clear that the attempt on behalf of the Jews to abandon their Jewish identity would have only limited success. Significantly, the Berlin Anti-Semitism Debate involving the historian Heinrich von Treitschke occurred during the Whilhelminian era that is often idealized. Other anti-Semitic groups and activities such as the "Anti-Semites League" founded by Wilhelm Marr, the "Christian Socialist Workers Party" established by the Protestant court preacher Adolf Stoecker, and the "Anti-Semites Petition" in the German Reichstag also took place during this promising era. This fateful trend was continued throughout World War I, only to gain momentum in the Weimar Republic. The assassination of Foreign Minister Walther Rathenau in 1922 and the anti-Semitic riots in the Scheunenviertel in 1923, were sad harbingers of what was to come under National Socialism.

Different religious interpretations, such as reform Judaism and neo-orthodoxy, also developed during the German Empire. After liberal Judaism established itself as the main form of Judaism practiced by Jews in and beyond Berlin in the 1860s, a minority of orthodox Jews responded by establishing an independent congregation in Berlin in 1869. They practiced a more conservative form of Judaism and called themselves the "Law-abiding Jewish religious society of Adass-Yisroel." Having failed to establish the research of Judaism as an independent discipline at the university, both the liberal and orthodox congregations grounded their intellectual and spiritual beliefs in scholarship conducted at private educational centers. The liberal "Advanced School for the Science of Judaism" was founded in 1872. The orthodox Rabbinical Seminary was established a year later.

nicht gelungen war, die Erforschung des Judentums an den Universitäten als eigenständige Disziplin einzuführen. Im Jahre 1872 wurde die liberale »Hochschule für die Wissenschaft des Judentums« gegründet und ein Jahr später das orthodoxe Rabbinerseminar.

Um die Jahrhundertwende bildete sich der politische Zionismus heraus, der schnell in Berlin ein Zentrum seiner Aktivitäten fand. So wurde beispielsweise das von Max Nordau propagierte Programm vom »Muskeljudentum« in jüdischen Turn- und Sportvereinen umgesetzt. In Reaktion auf die wachsende antisemitische Ausgrenzung wurden eigene Studentenverbindungen und Pfadfindergruppen gegründet. Ausdruck der beginnenden Emanzipationsbewegung von Frauen war die Gründung verschiedener zionistischer Frauenorganisationen und -vereine. Daneben wurde auch die landwirtschaftliche und handwerkliche Ausbildung gefördert, die der Vorbereitung auf die Einwanderung in Palästina diente.

Den Ersten Weltkrieg erlebten die meisten Juden als glühende deutsche Patrioten. Über 12 000 jüdische Soldaten kamen ums Leben. Ende 1916 wurde den antisemitischen Forderungen nachgegeben und die sogenannte »Judenzählung« durchgeführt, um die Beteiligung jüdischer Soldaten am Krieg zu untersuchen. Die Zählung, die eine überdurchschnittliche Beteiligung von Juden, gemessen an ihrem Anteil an der Bevölkerung, ergab, wurde allerdings nicht veröffentlicht. Um den auch nach dem Krieg anhaltenden antisemitischen Vorwurf der »Drückebergerei der Juden« zu widerlegen und sich vor ähnlichen Angriffen zu schützen, wurde 1919 der »Reichsbund jüdischer Frontsoldaten« in Berlin gegründet.

In den 1920er Jahren kam es einerseits zu einer Renaissance jüdischer Kultur, die sich in Literatur, Theater, Musik, bildender Kunst und Wissenschaft zeigte. Gleichzeitig verschärften sich die Aktivitäten radikaler antisemitischer Gruppierungen und Parteien, vor allem der NSDAP. Die Erschütterungen der Inflation, der Weltwirtschaftskrise und der Massenarbeitslosigkeit verschonten auch die Juden Berlins nicht. Der zunehmenden Verarmung der bürgerlichen Mittelschicht stellten sich die Jüdische

Political Zionism which developed at the turn of the century soon established its center in Berlin. Jewish gymnastics and sports clubs, for example, adopted "muscle Judaism," a program propagated by Max Nordau. In response to increasing anti-Semitic discrimination, independent Jewish student associations and Boy Scout groups were founded. The emergence of a women's emancipation movement also found expression in various Zionist women's organizations and associations. At the same time Zionists encouraged agricultural and artisan training as preparation for immigration to Palestine.

Most Jews embraced the outbreak of the First World War as fervent German patriots. More than 12,000 Jewish soldiers ended up losing their lives in the Great War. At the end of 1916 the military gave in to anti-Semitic demands by carrying out a "Jewish census" to determine how many Jewish soldiers were involved in the war. The census found that given their percentage within the larger population, Jews were over-proportionately represented in the military, but the results were never published. The "Reich Federation of Jewish Front Soldiers" was established in Berlin in 1919 in response to the persistent accusation that Jews had "shirked their duty" during the war. The federation tried to counter and protect against these and other slanderous attacks.

Jewish culture underwent a renaissance in the 1920s which found expression in literature, theater, music, art and science. But the activities of radical anti-Semitic groups and parties, above all the NSDAP, also gained in strength in these years. At the same time Jews in Berlin were not spared the duress caused by inflation, economic crises and widespread unemployment. The Jewish community and private individuals responded to the increased impoverishment of the bourgeois middle class by establishing homes for the elderly and other social institutions and by engaging in charity activities.

The architecture and interiors of the large synagogues and community institutions that were erected during this time reflect the diversity of German Judaism and its different religious forms. The neo-Romantic synagogues tucked away from the street within a back courtyard are

Gemeinde und privates Engagement durch den Ausbau von Altersheimen und Sozialeinrichtungen sowie karitativen Initiativen entgegen.

Die Architektur und Ausstattung der in diesem Zeitraum errichteten großen Synagogen und Gemeinde-Einrichtungen spiegelt die Vielfalt der verschiedenen Strömungen des deutschen Judentums wider. Typisch für die Kaiserzeit waren die von der Straßenseite abgewandten, neoromanischen Hinterhofsynagogen. Als Zeichen gewachsenen Selbstbewusstseins entstanden später auch freistehende, repräsentative Gemeindesynagogen. Aufgrund der Zerstörungen in der Reichspogromnacht und dem Zweiten Weltkrieg sind die meisten dieser Bauten nicht mehr erhalten, und nur noch Photographien zeugen von dieser Vergangenheit.

Berühmte jüdische Persönlichkeiten wie Albert Einstein, Walther Rathenau und Max Liebermann werden in diesem Buch genauso abgebildet wie die sogenannten einfachen Leute. Jüdisches Leben wird in Aufnahmen von Hochzeiten, Bar-Mizwa-Feiern, Schabbatfeiern und anderen religiösen Festtagen eingefangen. Die großen Warenhäuser, Geschäfte und Restaurants, z.B. von Tietz, Jandorf und Kempinski, prägten das quirlige Großstadtleben ebenso, wie es die kleinen Läden jüdischer Händler im Scheunenviertel taten. Eine Auswahl von Photographien aus jüdischen Ausbildungsstätten und Sozialeinrichtungen rundet dieses Bild ab.

Der Zeitrahmen des vorliegenden Bandes umspannt die Anfänge der Photographie bis zur ersten Blütezeit des Photojournalismus in den 1920er Jahren. Die Aufnahmen stammen sowohl von bekannten als auch von unbekannten Photographen. Neben professionellen Porträts und Architekturphotographien sowie journalistischen Aufnahmen wurden auch private Familienbilder und amateurhafte Schnappschüsse ausgewählt. Ein besonderes Augenmerk galt den Zeugnissen alltäglichen und religiösen jüdischen Lebens. So ergibt sich ein breites Spektrum zwischen inszenierter Pose und zufälligem Einblick, zwischen Selbstdarstellung und Authentizität. Der angegebene Zeitraum wird hier mitunter großzügig aufgefasst, da auf der einen Seite nicht alle Photos datiert sind bzw. unterschiedliche Angaben existieren und

typical of the German Empire. Later, detached, dignified community synagogues were erected as a sign of the community's growing confidence. Most of these structures were badly damaged during the Nazi-organized pogrom in November 1938 and by World War II and are no longer standing. This past is only preserved by photographs.

Famous Jews such as Albert Einstein, Walther Rathenau and Max Liebermann are portrayed in this book alongside men and women who were not famous. Jewish life is captured in photographs of weddings, Bar Mitzvah celebrations, Sabbath dinners and other religious holidays. The large department stores and restaurants owned by Tietz, Jandorf, Kempinski along with the smaller shops run by Jewish merchants in the Scheunenviertel had an important influence on the exciting life in the big city. A selection of photographs of Jewish educational centers and social institutions completes this presentation.

This book covers a period from the beginning of photography to the first zenith of photographic journalism in the 1920s. The photos were taken by both well-known and little-known photographers. The collection includes professional portraits, architectural photographs, journalistic shots as well as private family pictures and amateur snapshots. Special attention was paid to pictures revealing details of daily and religious Jewish life. The book thus contains pictures of a broad range of situations, ranging from staged poses to accidental shots, from self-presentation to authenticity.

The dates attributed to the photos are often vague because not all photos were dated and some had varying information. A decision was made to include a few photos taken before 1871 or right after the National Socialists took power because they seemed particularly well suited to the collection.

This book of photography builds on my travel guide, "Das jüdische Berlin. Kultur, Religion und Alltag gestern und heute" (which appeared in English under the title "Jewish Berlin. Culture, Religion, Daily Life Yesterday and Today"), which was also published by the Jaron Verlag. For those readers interested in learning more

auf der anderen Seite einige wenige Photos, die besonders geeignet erschienen, vor 1871 bzw. unmittelbar nach der nationalsozialistischen Machtübernahme entstanden sind.

Dieser Bildband ergänzt meinen Reiseführer »Das jüdische Berlin. Kultur, Religion und Alltag gestern und heute« (englisch: »Jewish Berlin. Culture, Religion, Daily Life Yesterday and Today«), der ebenfalls im Jaron Verlag erschienen ist. Wer die hier vorliegenden knappen Informationen aus den Bildunterschriften vertiefen möchte, dem sei dieses Taschenbuch empfohlen.

Mein Dank gilt einer Reihe von Menschen, ohne die dieser Band nicht zustande gekommen wäre. In jeder Hinsicht möchte ich an erster Stelle meinem Verleger Norbert Jaron danken, der von Anfang an dieses Buchprojekt weit- und umsichtig förderte. Besonders dankbar bin ich meinem Kollegen Aubrey Pomerance, dem Leiter des Leo Baeck Instituts Berlin, der mir unkompliziert Zugang zu seinen Datenbanken gewährte. Miriam Intrator vom Leo Baeck Institute New York bin ich zu Dank verpflichtet für ihr großzügiges Entgegenkommen bei der Bereitstellung der gewünschten Photographien. Von Herzen gedankt sei Franziska Bogdanov, die mir als Mitarbeiterin im Archiv des Jüdischen Museums Berlin äußerst kompetent und uneigennützig ihr biographisches Wissen über einzelne abgebildete Menschen zur Verfügung stellte. Last but not least ist dem Bildarchiv Preußischer Kulturbesitz und der Bildagentur akg-images zu danken, die einen Großteil der Abbildungen zur Verfügung stellten. Widmen möchte ich diesen Bildband Katrin Rebiger, weil sie mich lehrte, nicht nur mit den Augen zu sehen.

Berlin-Kreuzberg, im Juni 2008

about Jewish life in Berlin than what is provided by the brief captions here is invited to take a look at this paperback.

My thanks go to a number of people without whom this book would never have been possible. Foremost I would like to thank my publisher Norbert Jaron, who supported this book project wholeheartedly from the very beginning. I am also very grateful to my colleague Aubrey Pomerance, director of the Leo Baeck Institute in Berlin, who provided me easy access to his databanks. And I owe my thanks to Miriam Intrator from the Leo Baeck Institute in New York for her generous assistance in providing the requested photographs. A heartfelt thanks goes to Franziska Bogdanov, who works in the archive of the Berlin Jewish Museum and who was very competent and selfless in sharing her biographical knowledge of certain individuals who appear in these photos. Last but not least, my thanks go to the photo archive of the Preußischer Kulturbesitz (Prussian Cultural Heritage) and the photo agency akg-images which provided a large number of the photographs. I would like to dedicate this book to Katrin Rebiger who taught me to see with more than just my eyes.

Berlin-Kreuzberg, June 2008

Spielende Kinder auf dem Großen Jüdenhof in Berlin-Mitte. Der Name erinnerte bis zur Beseitigung dieses Platzes in der DDR-Zeit – wie auch die heute noch existierende benachbarte Jüdenstraße – an die mittelalterliche Ansiedlung von Juden in Berlin, die sich im Klosterviertel hinter dem Roten Rathaus konzentrierte. (1930)

Children playing in the Grosser Jüdenhof (large Jewish court) in Berlin-Mitte. The name of this plaza that was destroyed during the GDR era, like "Jüden strasse," a nearby street that still exists today, recalls a Jewish medieval settlement in Berlin that was concentrated in the cloister quarter behind the Red Town Hall. (1930)

Familie Loevinson mit sechs Kindern in Charlottenburg. Diese seltene Aufnahme einer assimilierten jüdischen Familie vor der Kaiserzeit stammt aus der Sammlung von Johanna Meyer geb. Loevinson (1874–1958), die in den 1920er und 1930er Jahren Radiosprecherin in Berlin war. (Sommer 1867)

The Loevinson family with their six children in Charlottenburg. This rare photograph of an assimilated family living before the German Empire is from the Johanna Meyer collection. Meyer, born Loevinson (1874–1958), had been a radio announcer in the 1920s and 1930s in Berlin. (Summer 1867)

Das Grab von Moses Mendelssohn (1729–1786) auf dem Jüdischen Friedhof an der Großen Hamburger Straße in Mitte. Der aus Dessau stammende Mendelssohn gilt als der Vater der jüdischen Aufklärung, die einerseits die bürgerliche Gleichstellung forderte und andererseits Juden Kultur und Wissenschaft der christlichen Umwelt nahebrachte. Das Photo zeigt den zweiten Grabstein, der 1896 ihm zu Ehren errichtet und 1941 von der Gestapo zerstört wurde. (1920)

The grave of Moses Mendelssohn (1729–1786) at the Jewish cemetery on Grosse Hamburger Strasse in Mitte. Mendelssohn, born in Dessau, is regarded as the father of the Jewish Enlightenment, a movement which called for equal rights to Jews as citizens while at the same time familiarizing Jews with Christian culture and science. The photo shows the second tombstone that was erected in his honor in 1896 and destroyed by the Gestapo in 1941. (1920)

Der Friedhof in der Großen Hamburger Straße ist der älteste Friedhof der neuzeitlichen Jüdischen Gemeinde in Berlin. Er wurde 1672 eingeweiht und 1827 aus Kapazitätsgründen geschlossen. 1872 zählte der damalige Friedhofsverwalter Leiser Landshuth in seinem Verzeichnis noch 2767 Grabsteine mit entzifferbaren Inschriften. Die Gestapo ließ den Friedhof 1943 zerstören, weil dort ein Splittergraben ausgehoben werden sollte. (Friedrich Seidenstücker, zwischen 1930 und 1935)

The cemetery located on Grosse Hamburger Strasse is the oldest cemetery of the modern Jewish community in Berlin. It opened in 1672 and was closed in 1827 when it ran out of space. In 1872 Leiser Landshuth, cemetery administrator at the time, recorded 2767 existing gravestones with decipherable inscriptions. The Gestapo completely destroyed the cemetery in 1943 in order to have a slit trench dug there. (Friedrich Seidenstücker, between 1930 and 1935)

Im Jahre 1856 wurde die barocke Alte Synagoge in der Heidereutergasse vom christlichen Baumeister und Schinkel-Schüler Eduard Knoblauch klassizistisch umgebaut. Im Zuge der Reform des jüdischen Gottesdienstes wurde dabei auch das Vorlesepult aus der Saalmitte nach vorne an den altarähnlichen Toraschrein gerückt. (Abraham Pisarek, um 1930)

The Old Baroque Synagogue on Heidereutergasse was remodeled into a Classical structure in 1856 by Eduard Knoblauch, a Christian architect and pupil of Schinkel. As Jewish prayer services underwent reform, the bima was also moved away from the center of the hall and closer to the altar-like Torah ark at the front. (Abraham Pisarek, c. 1930)

Eingang der Alten Synagoge in der Heidereutergasse (Mitte). Die älteste neuzeitliche Synagoge der Jüdischen Gemeinde Berlin wurde von Michael Kemmeter entworfen und 1714 eingeweiht. Sie wurde beim Novemberpogrom 1938 demoliert, im Zweiten Weltkrieg zerstört und in den 1960er Jahren abgerissen. Heute befindet sich an diesem Ort auf einer Grünfläche eine neu vermauerte Grundstücksecke und eine Informationstafel. (Abraham Pisarek, um 1930)

Entrance to the Old Synagogue on Heidereutergasse (Mitte). The Berlin Jewish community's oldest synagogue of the modern era, designed by Michael Kemmeter, opened in 1714. It was damaged during the November pogrom of 1938, destroyed in World War II and torn down in the sixties. Today a newly erected wall accompanied by an information panel stands on a green lawn at the corner of the property where the synagogue once stood. (Abraham Pisarek, c. 1930)

Der Rechtsanwalt und Politiker Eduard Lasker (1829–1884) war 1866 Mitbegründer und Vorsitzender der Nationalliberalen Partei, von 1862 bis 1879 Mitglied des Preußischen Abgeordnetenhauses und von 1871 bis 1884 des Deutschen Reichstages. Er teilt sich zusammen mit seinem Freund und Mitstreiter Ludwig Bamberger auf dem Jüdischen Friedhof Schönhauser Allee ein Doppelgrab.

The lawyer and politician Eduard Lasker (1829–1884) was co-founder and chairman of the National Liberal Party in 1866. He was a member of the Prussian House of Representatives from 1862 to 1879 and a representative of the German Reichstag from 1871 to 1884. He shares a double grave with Ludwig Bamberger, his friend and comrade-in-arms, at the Jewish cemetery on Schönhauser Allee.

Der 1848er Revolutionär, Bank- und Finanzberater Ludwig Bamberger (1823–1899) war zusammen mit seinem Freund Lasker 1866 Mitbegründer der Nationalliberalen Partei. Gemeinsam traten sie 1880 aus Protest gegen das Einlenken auf die restriktive Politik Bismarcks aus der Partei aus. Bamberger und Lasker waren an der Gesetzgebung von 1876 beteiligt, die den Austritt aus der Jüdischen Gemeinde ohne Konversion ermöglichte. (1871)

Ludwig Bamberger (1823–1899), 1848 revolutionary as well as bank and finance advisor, co-founded the National Liberal Party with his friend Lasker in 1866. They both left the party in 1880 in an act of protest against the party's willingness to accept Bismarck's restrictive policies. Bamberger and Lasker helped to establish the legislation of 1876 which allowed people who had not converted to leave the Jewish community. (1871)

Eingang des Tempels der Reformgemeinde in der Johannisstraße 16 (Mitte). Diese Synagoge wurde von Gustav Stier entworfen, 1854 eingeweiht, beim Novemberpogrom 1938 verwüstet, im Zweiten Weltkrieg zerstört und später abgerissen. Die Reformgemeinde führte den deutschsprachigen Gottesdienst sowie Orgel- und Chormusik ein und orientierte sich am Protestantismus. (Abraham Pisarek, um 1930)

Entrance to the Reform Congregation Temple at Johannisstrasse 16 (Mitte). This synagogue, designed by Gustav Stier, opened in 1854. It was vandalized during the November pogrom of 1938, destroyed in World War II and later torn down. The Reform Congregation introduced prayer services in German with organ and choral music accompaniment and was oriented towards Protestantism. (Abraham Pisarek, c. 1930)

Blick auf das Vorlesepult und den Toraschrein im Tempel der Reformgemeinde in der Johannisstraße 16. Hier predigte auch der erste Rabbiner der Reformgemeinde, Samuel Holdheim (1806–1860), dessen radikales Credo lautete: »Im Zeitalter des Talmuds hatte der Talmud Recht. In meiner Zeit habe ich Recht.« Zu den Neuerungen gehörte auch, dass die Gottesdienste am Sonntag (!) stattfanden und anstelle der Bar-Mizwa-Feier für Knaben eine Einsegnung für Jungen und Mädchen gefeiert wurde. (Abraham Pisarek, um 1930)

View of the bima and Torah ark in the Temple of the Reform Congregation at Johannisstrasse 16. Samuel Holdheim (1806–1860), the first rabbi of the Reform Congregation, preached here. He was known for his radical creed: "In the age of the Talmud, the Talmud is right. In my age, I am right." Changes introduced included Sunday prayer services and a consecration ceremony for both boys and girls which replaced the traditional Bar Mitzvah celebration for young Jewish boys. (Abraham Pisarek, c. 1930)

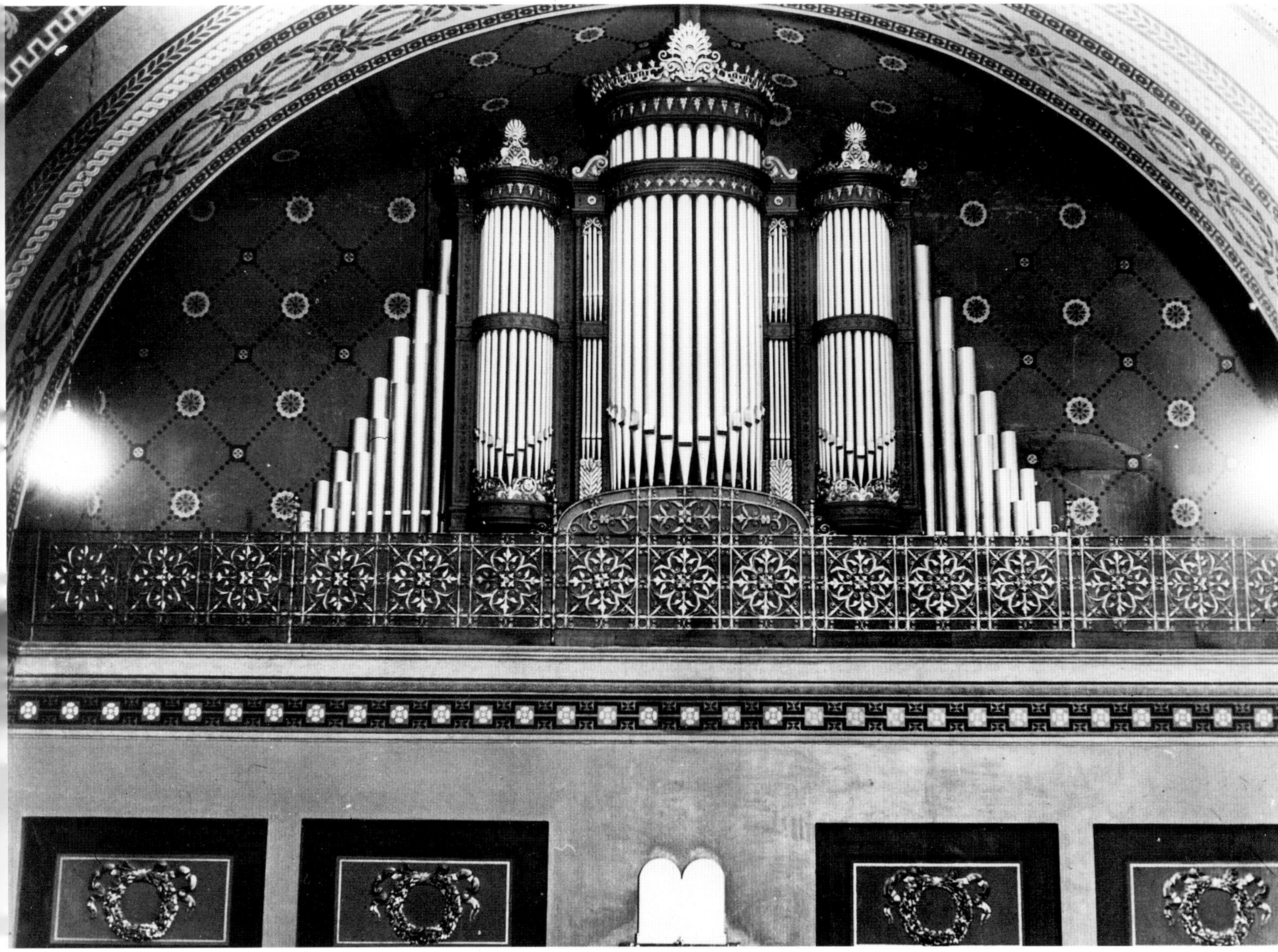

Orgel über dem Toraschrein im Tempel der Reformgemeinde in der Johannisstraße 16. Die Einführung der Orgelmusik war eine der grundlegenden und umstrittensten Neuerungen der jüdischen Reformbewegung, die sich seit dem Anfang des 19. Jahrhunderts auch in Berlin formierte.

Organ above the Torah ark in the Temple of the Reform Congregation at Johannisstrasse 16. Using organ music at prayer services was one of the fundamental and controversial changes introduced by the Jewish reform movement. The movement originated in the early 19th century and was strongly influential in Berlin.

Nachdem der Historiker Leopold Zunz (1794–1886) von 1815 bis 1819 an der Universität Berlin studiert hatte, gründete er zusammen mit Eduard Gans den »Verein für Cultur und Wissenschaft der Juden«. Er gab eine wissenschaftliche Zeitschrift heraus und verfasste vor allem literaturgeschichtliche Artikel und Bücher zum Judentum. Zunz wurde auf dem Jüdischen Friedhof Schönhauser Allee beerdigt. (Julius Löwensohn, 1869)

After studying at the Berlin University from 1815 to 1819, the historian Leopold Zunz (1794–1886) founded the "Association of Jewish Culture and Science" with Eduard Gans. He published a scholarly journal and wrote mostly literary history articles and books on Judaism. Zunz was buried at the Jewish cemetery at Schönhauser Allee. (Julius Löwensohn, 1869)

Innenansicht der Neuen Synagoge in der Oranienburger Straße 29 (Mitte) mit Blick auf Vorlesepult und Toraschrein. Die damals größte Synagoge Deutschlands bot 1800 Männern und 1200 Frauen Platz. Die reiche dekorative Innenausstattung, das raffinierte Licht und Konzerte zogen auch nichtjüdische Besucher an. An die zerstörte und abgetragene Haupthalle erinnert heute nur noch eine Umrissmarkierung auf dem freigelassenen Hinterhof des Centrum Judaicum. (Um 1885)

Interior of the New Synagogue at Oranienburger Strasse 29 (Mitte) with a view of the bima and Torah ark. It was the largest synagogue in Germany at the time, providing seating for 1800 men and 1200 women. The richly decorated interior, the artful lighting and musical concerts also drew non-Jewish visitors. An outline on the open courtyard behind Centrum Judaicum is all that recalls the main hall of the synagogue that was destroyed and later removed from the site. (c. 1885)

Rabbiner Abraham Geiger (1810–1874) war ein bedeutender Streiter für das Reformjudentum. Nachdem er als Rabbiner in Wiesbaden, Breslau und Frankfurt a.M. wirkte, wurde er 1870 nach Berlin an die Neue Synagoge berufen. Er war an der Gründung der Hochschule für die Wissenschaft des Judentums beteiligt und lehrte dort. Sein Grab befindet sich auf dem Friedhof Schönhauser Allee. (Bildarchiv Pisarek, um 1865)

Rabbi Abraham Geiger (1810–1874) was an important supporter of Reform Judaism. After serving as a rabbi in Wiesbaden, Breslau and Frankfurt a.M., he was appointed to the New Synagogue in Berlin in 1870. He helped to found the Advanced School for the Science of Judaism and also taught there. He is buried at the Jewish cemetery at Schönhauser Allee. (Pisarek Photo Archive, c. 1865)

Repräsentantensaal der Neuen Synagoge. Alle wahlberechtigten Gemeindemitglieder wählten die Repräsentantenversammlung, die wiederum unter allen Gemeindemitgliedern die Mitglieder des Gemeindevorstandes auswählte. Der Repräsentantensaal befindet sich im vorderen Gebäudeteil der Synagoge, der heute, rekonstruiert, im Centrum Judaicum besichtigt werden kann. (Hermann Rückwardt, 1885)

The Representative Hall of the New Synagogue. The congregation members who were eligible to vote elected the representative assembly, which in turn selected congregation members to serve on the community board. The Representative Hall was located in the front section of the synagogue building, which has been rebuilt and can be viewed today from inside Centrum Judaicum. (Hermann Rückwardt, 1885)

Antisemiten sahen in dem orientalisch wirkenden Prunkbau der Neuen Synagoge ein Indiz für die von ihnen behauptete Fremdheit und den angeblichen Reichtum der Juden. So schreibt z.B. der Historiker Heinrich von Treitschke im Jahre 1879: »Erwägt man die charakteristische Tatsache, dass das schönste und prächtigste Gotteshaus der deutschen Hauptstadt eine Synagoge ist – was natürlich nicht den Juden, sondern den Christen zum Vorwurfe gereicht –, so lässt sich schlechterdings nicht in Abrede stellen, dass die Juden in Deutschland mächtiger sind als in irgend einem Lande Westeuropas.« (Dittmar Schweitzer, Anfang 20. Jahrhundert)

Anti-Semites regarded the magnificent Oriental-style architecture of the New Synagogue as evidence of what they believed to be the foreignness and alleged wealth of the Jews. The historian Heinrich von Treitschke, for example, wrote in 1879: "Given the characteristic fact that the most beautiful and magnificent house of prayer in the capital is a synagogue – for which the Christians, not the Jews, no less are criticized – it is difficult to dismiss the claim that the Jews in Germany are more powerful than in any other West European country." (Dittmar Schweitzer, beginning of the 20th century)

OSCAR ROLOFF HOF-PHOTOGRAPH
Sr. Königl. Hoheit des regierenden Großherzogs von
Mecklenburg-Schwerin u. d. reg. Fürsten v. Schwarzburg-Rudolstadt.
Jnhaber d. np. gold. Medaille für Kunst u. Wissenschaft.
BERLIN, W. Unter den Linden 24.
zwischen Hofconditor Kranzler und der Passage.

Nachdem alle Bemühungen, die Wissenschaft des Judentums als universitäre Disziplin zu etablieren, gescheitert waren, entschied man sich 1872 zur Einrichtung einer privaten Bildungsstätte, der Hochschule für die Wissenschaft des Judentums. Ab 1907 fand der Unterricht in einem Neubau in der Artilleriestraße 14 (heute Tucholskystraße 9, Mitte) statt, den Johann Höniger entworfen hatte. (1930er Jahre)

After all efforts to establish the Science of Judaism as a university discipline failed, a private educational center called the Advanced School for the Science of Judaism was established in 1872. Beginning in 1907 classes were held in a new building designed by Johann Höniger at Artilleriestrasse 14 (today's Tucholskystrasse 9 in Mitte). (1930s)

Franz Oppenheimer (1864–1943) als Student mit zwei Kommilitonen in der Uniform einer schlagenden Studentenverbindung. Der Arzt, Nationalökonom und Soziologe gründete 1911 eine Siedlungsgenossenschaft in Merchawiah, Palästina. Von 1919 bis 1929 hatte Oppenheimer eine Professur in Frankfurt a.M. Im Jahre 1938 emigrierte er über Japan in die USA, wo er in Los Angeles verstarb. (Hof-Photograph Oscar Roloff, ca. 1885)

Franz Oppenheimer (1864–1943) and two fellow-students wearing the uniform of a fencing fraternity. The doctor, economist and sociologist founded a housing cooperative in Merchawiah, Palestine in 1911. Oppenheimer held a professorship in Frankfurt a.M. from 1919 to 1929. He immigrated by way of Japan to the United States in 1938 and died in Los Angeles. (Court photographer Oscar Roloff, c. 1885)

Die engagierte Sozialarbeiterin Lina Morgenstern (1830–1909) gründete eine Reihe von Volksküchen und war daher in Berlin als »Suppen-Lina« sehr populär. Sie setzte sich auch für die Rettung verwahrloster Mädchen und für die Ausbildung von Arbeiterinnen ein. Ihr Grab befindet sich auf dem Jüdischen Friedhof Weißensee.

The dedicated social worker Lina Morgenstern (1830–1909) founded a number of soup kitchens which is why she was known as "Soup Lina" and very popular in Berlin. She also spoke up for saving neglected girls and educating female workers. She is buried at the Jewish cemetery in Weissensee.

Wohnhaus Gerson von Bleichröders (1822–1893) und väterliches Bankgebäude in der Behrenstraße 61-63 (Mitte). Bleichröder war Hofbankier Kaiser Wilhelms I. und persönlicher Berater Otto von Bismarcks. Für seine Verdienste bei der Finanzierung des preußisch-österreichischen Krieges und bei der Abwicklung der französischen Reparationszahlungen wurde er als erster nichtgetaufter Jude in Preußen in den Adelsstand erhoben. 1938 wurde sein Bankhaus von den Nationalsozialisten »arisiert«. (F. Albert Schwartz, 1889)

Home of the banker Gerson von Bleichröder (1822–1893) and the bank building established by his father at Behrenstrasse 61-63 (Mitte). Bleichröder was the court banker of Kaiser Wilhelm I and the personal advisor of Otto von Bismarck. In recognition of his services in financing the Prussian-Austrian wars and in handling the French reparations payments he became the first non-baptized Jew to be elevated to the hereditary peerage in Prussia. His bank was "aryanized" by the National Socialists in 1938. (F. Albert Schwartz, 1889)

Mitglieder des Russisch-jüdischen wissenschaftlichen Vereins im Jahre 1890. Der Verein war zwei Jahre zuvor in Berlin gegründet worden, um in Deutschland studierenden Russen Judentum und Zionismus zu vermitteln. Zu seinen Mitgliedern gehörte auch der spätere israelische Präsident Chaim Weizmann. In der vorderen Reihe, sitzend in der Mitte, der einzige deutsche Jude im Verein: Heinrich Loewe (1869 Wandsleben – 1951 Haifa).

Members of the Russian-Jewish scholarly association in 1890. The association was founded two years earlier in Berlin to teach Russians who were studying in Germany about Judaism and Zionism. Chaim Weizmann, who would later become president of Israel, was also one of its members. Heinrich Loewe (1869 Wandsleben – 1951 Haifa), seated in the middle of the front row, was the only German Jew in the association.

Der Literaturwissenschaftler Ludwig Geiger (1848–1919), Sohn von Abraham Geiger, war Professor an der Berliner Universität und arbeitete vor allem zu Goethe und zur Renaissance. Maßgeblich waren seine bearbeiteten Nachauflagen von Jacob Burckhardts »Kultur der Renaissance«. Daneben ist auch seine »Geschichte der Juden in Berlin« bis heute ein Standardwerk. Sein Grab befindet sich auf dem Jüdischen Friedhof Schönhauser Allee. (J.C. Schaarwächter, 1891)

The literary scholar Ludwig Geiger (1848–1919), son of Abraham Geiger, was a professor at the Berlin University specializing in the works of Goethe and the Renaissance period. His edited reprints of Jacob Burckhardt's "Culture of Renaissance" were decisive works. Another study, "The History of Jews in Berlin" also remains a standard work today. His grave is located at the Jewish cemetery at Schönhauser Allee. (J.C. Schaarwächter, 1891)

Innenansicht der Synagoge Lindenstraße 48-50. Typisch für den liberalen Ritus ist die Anordnung des Vorlesepults direkt vor dem Toraschrein und der Einbau einer Orgel. In der Pogromnacht 1938 wurde die Einrichtung der Synagoge demoliert. In der Folgezeit diente diese als Getreidespeicher. (Abraham Pisarek)

View inside the synagogue at Lindenstrasse 48-50. The placement of the bima directly in front of the Torah ark and the built-in organ are typical of liberal Judaism. The interior of the synagogue was vandalized in the 1938 pogrom. Afterwards it was used as a warehouse for storing grain. (Abraham Pisarek)

Die Synagoge in der Lindenstraße 48-50 (heute Axel-Springer-Straße, Kreuzberg) wurde vom Architektenbüro Cremer & Wolffenstein im neoromanischen Stil entworfen und 1891 eingeweiht. Der Backsteinbau der im Zweiten Weltkrieg zerstörten und 1956 abgerissenen liberalen Synagoge befand sich einst im Hinterhof, woran heute eine Installation von Zvi Hecker, Micha Ullman und Eyal Weizman erinnert. (Abraham Pisarek, um 1930)

The synagogue at Lindenstrasse 48-50 (today's Axel-Springer-Strasse, Kreuzberg) was designed in a neo-Romanesque style by the architecture office Cremer & Wolffenstein and dedicated in 1891. The brick building that was destroyed in World War II and torn down in 1956 was set in the back courtyard. Today an installation by Zvi Hecker, Micha Ullman and Eyal Weizman commemorates the liberal synagogue that no longer exists. (Abraham Pisarek, c. 1930)

Der Student Walter Sally Simon (stehend, Zweiter von rechts) mit Kommilitonen der jüdischen Studentenverbindung »Fuchsia« im Sommersemester 1901. Weil Juden von den sich antisemitisch und deutschnational gebenden Studentenverbindungen ausgeschlossen wurden, gründeten sie ihre eigenen Vereine. (H. Zeidler)

Walter Sally Simon (standing second from the right) with fellow students of the Jewish fraternity "Fuchsia" during the summer semester of 1901. Since Jews were excluded from the increasingly anti-Semitic and German nationalistic student associations, they began to establish their own fraternities. (H. Zeidler)

Walter Sally Simon (1882–1942) als junger Student in der Uniform einer schlagenden Verbindung. Der in Berlin geborene Rechtsanwalt war mit Helene Hahn (1886–1942) verheiratet. Die Eheleute wurden 1942 nach Riga deportiert und dort wahrscheinlich ermordet. Ihre beiden Kinder Carla und Stefan Helmut konnten nach England fliehen. (Atelier Wertheim, 1900)

Walter Sally Simon (1882–1942) as a young student in the uniform of a fencing fraternity. The attorney, born in Berlin, was married to Helene Hahn (1886–1942). The couple was deported to Riga in 1942 and presumably murdered there. Their two children Carla and Stefan Helmut were able to flee to England. (Atelier Wertheim, 1900)

Der Bankier und Kaufmann James Henry Simon (1851–1932) finanzierte Ausgrabungen in Jericho, Babylon und Tell Amarna. Die wertvollen Funde, darunter die Büste der Nofretete, sowie seine Sammlung italienischer Renaissancekunst schenkte er den Berliner Museen. Simon war auch karitativ tätig und gründete bzw. finanzierte u.a. den Verein zum Schutze der Kinder vor Ausnutzung und Misshandlung, den Verein für Volksbäder und den Hilfsverein der deutschen Juden. (Rudolf Dührkoop, 1915)

The banker and salesman James Henry Simon (1851–1932) financed the excavations of Jericho, Babylon and Tell Amarna. He donated the valuable objects found – such as the bust of Nofretete – and his Italian Renaissance art collection to Berlin museums. Simon was also involved in charity and supported many institutions including The Association to Protect Children from Exploitation and Mistreatment, The Public Bathing Club and the Benevolent Society of the German Jews. (Rudolf Dührkoop, 1915)

Die Vereinigung Jüdischer Studierender zu Berlin wurde 1895 von Heinrich Loewe und Max Bodenheimer gegründet. Ihre Aufgabe war die Pflege und Verbreitung jüdischer Kultur, als Reaktion auf den antisemitischen Verein Deutscher Studenten. Typisch waren auch hier Bräuche studentischer Verbindungen wie Kneipengeselligkeit, Zechereien, Fechtduelle, Vereinsfarben, Fahnen, Schärpen und Mützen.

Heinrich Loewe and Max Bodenheimer founded the Fraternity of Jewish Students in Berlin in 1895. Its aim was to preserve and spread Jewish culture, particularly in response to the anti-Semitic Association of German Students. They carried on many of the traditions typical of student fraternities: socializing in bars, carousing, fencing duels, club colors, flags, sashes and caps.

Das Warenhaus Jandorf in der Belle-Alliance-Straße 1/2. Im Zweiten Weltkrieg wurde das Gebäude zerstört. Der Unternehmer Adolf Jandorf (1870–1932) eröffnete 1892 am Spittelmarkt (Mitte) sein erstes Warenhaus nach amerikanischem Vorbild, dem noch fünf weitere folgen sollten, darunter das Kaufhaus des Westens (KaDeWe). Der Hermann-Tietz-Konzern übernahm im Jahre 1926 alle Jandorf-Kaufhäuser. (Um 1905)

The Jandorf department store at Belle-Alliance-Strasse 1/2. The building was destroyed in World War II. The entrepreneur Adolf Jandorf (1870–1932) opened his first department store, modeled after the ones in America, in 1892 at Spittelmarkt (Mitte). He later established five more, including the Kaufhaus des Westens (KaDeWe). The Hermann Tietz group took over all the Jandorf stores in 1926. (c. 1905)

Mitglieder des Jüdischen Turnvereins Bar Kochba Berlin im Jahre 1902. Der Verein wurde 1898 in Berlin von 48 jungen Juden gegründet. Bereits 1903 zählte er vierhundert Mitglieder. In der eigenen »Jüdischen Turnzeitung« hieß es programmatisch: »Wir wollen dem schlaffen jüdischen Leib die verlorene Spannkraft wiedergeben, ihn frisch und kräftig, gewandt und stark machen.«

Members of Bar Kochba Berlin, the Jewish gymnastics club in 1902. The club was founded in Berlin in 1898 by 48 young Jews. It already had four hundred members by 1903. Its own "Jewish Gymnastics Newspaper" proclaimed: "We want to give the flabby Jewish body back its lost resilience, invigorating it and making it athletic, adroit and strong."

J.T.V.B.K.

Stammhaus der Leinenweberei Julius Bendix & Söhne am Neuen Markt 1-2 (Mitte). Die Berliner Textilbranche war bis in die Zeit des Nationalsozialismus stark von jüdischen Konfektionären und Unternehmern geprägt. Heute erinnert eine mehrteilige Installation von Rainer Görß vor dem Eingang zum U-Bahnhof Hausvogteiplatz an diesen Beitrag zur Wirtschaftsgeschichte Berlins. (Ca. 1915)

Main offices of the Julius Bendix & Sons linen mill at Neuen Markt 1-2 (Mitte). The Berlin textile industry was dominated strongly by Jewish manufacturers and entrepreneurs until the National Socialist came to power. Today a multi-part installation by Rainer Görss at the entrance to the Hausvogteiplatz subway station recalls this important contribution to Berlin economic history. (c. 1915)

Der Bund Jüdischer Corporationen auf dem Gründungskartelltag in Berlin im Jahre 1901. In der dritten Reihe, Dritter von links: Martin Buber. Der Bund wurde als Dachorganisation gegründet, nachdem in mehreren Städten Vereine jüdischer Studenten entstanden waren. Im Jahre 1908 war der Bund die größte jüdische Studentenorganisation Deutschlands mit ca. 450 Mitgliedern. Bedeutende deutsche Zionisten wie Heinrich Loewe, Kurt Blumenfeld und Adolf Friedemann waren Mitglieder.

The Federation of Jewish Fraternities at the cartel founding congress in Berlin in 1901. Martin Buber is seen in the third row, third from the left. The federation was founded as an umbrella organization after many cities established Jewish student associations. The federation with approximately 450 members in 1908 was the largest Jewish student organization in Germany. Its members included important German Zionists such as Heinrich Loewe, Kurt Blumenfeld and Adolf Friedemann.

Die Hinterhofsynagoge in der Lützowstraße 16 (Tiergarten) wurde von Cremer & Wolffenstein im neogotischen Stil entworfen und 1898 eingeweiht, im Zweiten Weltkrieg zerstört und 1954 abgerissen. Eine Gedenktafel an einem Neubau erinnert heute an das einstige Gotteshaus. (Abraham Pisarek, um 1930)

The synagogue in the back courtyard of Lützowstrasse 16 (Tiergarten) was designed in a neo-Gothic style by Cremer & Wolffenstein and dedicated in 1898. It was destroyed in World War II and torn down in 1954. Today a memorial plaque on a new building recalls the house of prayer that once stood here. (Abraham Pisarek, c. 1930)

Auf einem Hinterhof wurde 1903/04 auch die Synagoge in der Rykestraße 53 (Prenzlauer Berg) errichtet. Das von Johann Höniger entworfene Gebäude, zu DDR-Zeiten die einzige Synagoge der Ost-Berliner Jüdischen Gemeinde, Anfang des 21. Jahrhunderts umfassend saniert, fasst 2000 Besucher. Das Photo zeigt den reich ornamentierten Hauptbogen über dem Toraschrein. (Um 1935)

The massive synagogue was erected in 1903/04 in the back courtyard of Rykestrasse 53 (Prenzlauer Berg). The building, designed by Johann Höniger, was the East Berlin Jewish community's only synagogue during the GDR era. It was reconstructed in the early 21st century and accommodates 2000 visitors today. The picture shows the richly ornamented chief arch above the Torah ark. (c. 1935)

Innenansicht des Lichthofes vom Warenhaus Tietz in der Leipziger Straße. Mit niedrigen und zugleich festen Preisen, einem breiten Sortiment an Waren, geschickter Werbung, Aktionswochen und immer prächtigeren Kaufhäusern gelang dem Inhaber Oscar Tietz der geschäftliche Durchbruch. Im Jahre 1934 wurde das Unternehmen zwangsweise »arisiert« und in »Hertie« umbenannt. (Postkarte, um 1910)

View inside the atrium of the Tietz department store on Leipziger Strasse. The owner Oscar Tietz achieved his commercial breakthrough with low and fixed prices, a wide assortment of goods, clever advertising, special promotions and the department store buildings that were always magnificent. The business was forced to "aryanize" in 1934 and renamed "Hertie." (Postcard, c. 1910)

Die Gründer des Jüdischen Verlags 1902 in Berlin. Stehend von links: der Graphiker Ephraim Moshe Lilien, der Chemiker und spätere israelische Präsident Chaim Weizmann, der zionistische Politiker David Trietsch; sitzend: der Schriftsteller Berthold Feiwel und der Religionsphilosoph Martin Buber.

Founders of the Jewish Publishing House in 1902 in Berlin. Standing from the left: The graphic artist Ephraim Moshe Lilien, the chemist and later president of Israel Chaim Weizmann, the Zionist politician David Trietsch; seated: the writer Berthold Feiwel and the religious philosopher Martin Buber.

Abraham Berliner (1833–1915) war Professor am orthodoxen Rabbinerseminar der neo-orthodoxen Adass-Jisroel-Gemeinde. Er unterrichtete Jüdische Geschichte und Literatur, arbeitete zeitweilig auch als Bibliothekar, edierte mittelalterliche Kommentarliteratur und forschte zur Geschichte der Juden in Rom. Das Seminar wurde 1873 gegründet und war ab 1904 in der Artilleriestraße 31 (heute Tucholskystraße 40, Mitte) untergebracht. (M. Kalischer)

Abraham Berliner (1833–1915) was a professor at the orthodox rabbinical seminary of the neo-orthodox Adass Yisroel congregation. He taught Jewish history and literature, worked for a time as librarian, edited medieval commentary literature and conducted research on the history of Jews in Rome. The seminary, founded in 1873, moved to Artilleriestrasse 31 (today's Tucholskystrasse 40, Mitte) in 1904. (M. Kalischer)

Die in der Luisenstadt wohnenden Juden gründeten 1872 einen Verein, der sich etwas später »Ahawas Reim. Louisenstädtischer Brüderverein« nannte. Dieser Verein richtete im Jahre 1879 in einem ehemaligen Fabrikgebäude im Hinterhof Prinzenstraße 86 (Kreuzberg) seine erste private Synagoge ein. Bis zu 350 Männer und Frauen konnten hier den Gottesdienst besuchen. (Atelier Wertheim, Pessach 1910)

The Jews living in Luisenstadt founded an association in 1872 that was later named "Ahawas Reim. Louisenstädtischer Brüderverein." In 1879 this association set up its first private synagogue in a former factory building located in the back courtyard of Prinzenstrasse 86 (Kreuzberg). There was room for 350 men and women to attend prayer services here. (Wertheim Studio, Passover 1910)

Familiengrab Ullstein auf dem Jüdischen Friedhof Schönhauser Allee. Der in Fürth geborene Leopold Ullstein (1826–1899) gründete 1877 in Berlin einen Verlag, in dem die »Berliner Zeitung« (später »B.Z. am Mittag«) erschien. Von 1871 bis 1877 war er als Vertreter der Freisinnigen Partei Stadtverordneter. Die von seinen fünf Söhnen herausgegebene »Berliner Morgenpost« war zeitweilig die auflagenstärkste deutsche Tageszeitung. Das expressionistische Ullstein-Haus am Mariendorfer Damm 1 (Tempelhof) wurde 1927 als Druckerei fertiggestellt. (2005)

The Ullstein family grave at the Jewish cemetery at Schönhauser Allee. Leopold Ullstein (1826–1899) was born in Fürth and founded a publishing house in Berlin in 1877 which printed the newspaper "Berliner Zeitung" (later called "B.Z. am Mittag"). He represented the Liberal Party as city councilor from 1871 to 1877. The "Berliner Morgenpost," published by his five sons, was for a time the German daily with the highest circulation. The expressionist Ullstein-Haus at Mariendorfer Damm 1 (Tempelhof) was built in 1927 as the publisher's printing house. (2005)

Der Verleger Rudolf Mosse (1843–1920, Zweiter von rechts) mit seinen Brüdern. Ab 1872 erschien im Mosse-Verlag, der sich zu einem Branchenriesen entwickelte, das liberale »Berliner Tageblatt«, später auch die »Berliner Morgenzeitung«, die »Berliner Volkszeitung« u.a. Mosse war Mitglied der Repräsentantenversammlung der Jüdischen Gemeinde und Vorsteher der Reformgemeinde in der Johannisstraße. Das Familiengrab der Mosses befindet sich auf dem Jüdischen Friedhof Weißensee. (1891)

The publisher Rudolf Mosse (1843–1920, second from the right) with his brothers. By 1872 the Mosse publishing house, a major player in the newspaper industry, was putting out a number of publications including the liberal "Berliner Tageblatt," and later the "Berliner Morgenzeitung" and the "Berliner Volkszeitung." Mosse was a member of the representative assembly of the Jewish community and head of the Reform Congregation on Johannisstrasse. The Mosse family mausoleum is located at the Jewish cemetery in Weissensee. (1891)

Der Verein Jüdischer Studenten Maccabaea wurde 1906 von dem späteren israelischen Justizminister Felix Rosenblüth (Mitte, mit Schärpe), Arthur Biram und Kurt Blumenfeld in Berlin gegründet. Maccabaea war der maßgebliche Verein innerhalb des Bundes Jüdischer Corporationen. Blumenfeld setzte sich erfolgreich für eine Wende vom theoretischen zum praktischen Zionismus mit dem Ziel der Übersiedlung nach Palästina ein.

The Jewish student association Maccabaea was founded in Berlin in 1906 by later Israeli minister of justice Felix Rosenblüth (in the middle with cap and sash), Arthur Biram and Kurt Blumenfeld. Maccabaea was the leading association within the Federation of Jewish Fraternities. Blumenfeld pushed successfully for a shift from theoretical to practical Zionism, which had the aim of resettling in Palestine.

Der zweigeschossige Kuppelbau der Vereinssynagoge im Hinterhof Münchener Straße 37 (Schöneberg) mit achthundert Sitzplätzen wurde 1910 eingeweiht. Hier wollten die Nationalsozialisten 1938 eine antijüdische Hetzausstellung mit geraubten Kultgegenständen veranstalten. Die im Zweiten Weltkrieg teilweise zerstörte Synagoge wurde 1956 abgerissen. 1963 wurde ein kubistischer Gedenkstein von Gerson Fehrenbach aufgestellt. (Abraham Pisarek, um 1930)

The two-story domed Synagogue Association building opened with seating for 800 in the back courtyard of Münchener Strasse 37 (Schöneberg) in 1910. The National Socialists planned to show an anti-Jewish propaganda exhibit here in 1938 with cultural objects stolen from the Jewish community. The synagogue, partly destroyed in World War II, was torn down in 1956. A cubist memorial stone created by Gerson Fehrenbach was erected in 1963 in memory of the synagogue. (Abraham Pisarek, c. 1930)

Innenansicht vom Erkersaal in den Weinstuben Kempinski in der Leipziger Straße. Berthold Kempinski (1845–1910) kam 1872 nach Berlin, um in der Friedrichstraße eine Weinhandlung zu eröffnen. Später folgten noch ein Weinversand-Geschäft, ein Delikatessengeschäft, ein Weinlager und ein Weinrestaurant. Das Grab des Firmengründers befindet sich auf dem Jüdischen Friedhof Weißensee. (Um 1910)

View of the bay window hall of the Kempinski wine tavern on Leipziger Strasse. Berthold Kempinski (1845–1910) came to Berlin in 1872 to open a wine store on Friedrichstrasse. He later also established a wine mail-order service, a delicatessen, a wine warehouse and wine restaurant. The entrepreneur is buried at the Jewish cemetery in Weissensee. (c. 1910)

Hasmonaea, die erste ausdrücklich zionistische Verbindung an der Berliner Universität, wurde 1902 von dem österreichischen Chemiestudenten Egon Rosenberg mit dem Ziel gegründet, in Palästina den Aufbau einer jüdischen »Heimstätte« zu unterstützen. Zu den Mitgliedern zählten Elias Auerbach, Georg Gerson und Richard Lichtheim. Schwesterverbindungen entstanden in München, Freiburg und Breslau. (1905)

The Zionist student association Hasmonaea in Berlin. The first explicitly Zionist association at the Berlin University was founded by the Austrian chemistry student Egon Rosenberg in 1902 to support the building of a Jewish "homestead" in Palestine. Its members included Elias Auerbach, Georg Gerson and Richard Lichtheim. Sister associations were established in Munich, Freiburg and Breslau. (1905)

Die Hinterhofsynagoge in der Pestalozzistraße 14 (Charlottenburg) wurde von Ernst Dorn im neoromanischen Stil entworfen und 1912 eingeweiht. Der Brand in der Pogromnacht 1938 konnte gelöscht werden. Die Synagoge, in der heute nach eigenem liberalem Ritus Gottesdienste mit Orgel- und Chormusik stattfinden, bietet 1400 Besuchern Platz. (Abraham Pisarek, 1925)

The synagogue in the back courtyard of Pestalozzistrasse 14 (Charlottenburg) was designed by the architect Ernst Dorn in a neo-Romanesque style and dedicated in 1912. The fire set to it during the 1938 pogrom was extinguished in time to save the building. The synagogue, which today conducts liberal services with organ and choir music, provides seating for 1400 worshipers. (Abraham Pisarek, 1925)

Der impressionistische Maler und Graphiker Lesser Ury (1861–1931), der zeitlebens im Schatten des einflussreicheren Max Liebermann stand, stammte aus Birnbaum in Posen und wohnte von 1888 bis zu seinem Tod am Nollendorfplatz. Von seinen Bildern werden heute besonders die regnerischen und abendlichen Berliner Straßenszenen geschätzt. Sein Grab liegt auf dem Friedhof Schönhauser Allee. (Um 1910)

The Impressionist painter and graphic designer Lesser Ury (1861–1931), who lived his entire life in the shadow of the more influential Max Liebermann, was born in Birnbaum in Posen and lived at Nollendorfplatz from 1888 until his death. His paintings of rainy scenes and evening street life in Berlin are especially admired today. His grave lies at the Schönhauser Allee cemetery. (c. 1910)

Die Synagoge Levetzowstraße 7/8 (Tiergarten) wurde vom Gemeindearchitekten Johann Höniger im neoklassizistischen Stil entworfen und 1914 eingeweiht. Sie bot den jüdischen Bewohnern Moabits über zweitausend Sitzplätze. Die Gottesdienste folgten dem liberalen Ritus. Die im Zweiten Weltkrieg beschädigte Synagoge wurde 1955/56 abgerissen. (Bildarchiv Pisarek, 1930)

The synagogue at Levetzowstrasse 7/8 (Tiergarten) was designed by the community's house architect Johann Höniger in a neo-Classical style and dedicated in 1914. It provided the residents of Moabit with 2000 seats. Prayer services were conducted according to the liberal tradition. The synagogue, damaged in World War II, was torn down in 1955/56. (Pisarek Photo Archive, 1930)

Hermann Cohen (1842–1918), Philosoph der Marburger Schule des Neukantianismus, zog nach seiner Emeritierung nach Berlin und widmete sich verstärkt dem Judentum. Hier unterrichtete er an der Hochschule für die Wissenschaft des Judentums und verfasste sein spätes Hauptwerk »Die Religion der Vernunft aus den Quellen des Judentums«. Cohen wurde auf dem Friedhof Schönhauser Allee beerdigt. (Bildarchiv Pisarek, um 1915)

Hermann Cohen (1842–1918), philosopher of the Marburg School of Neo-Kantianism, moved to Berlin after retirement and dedicated himself more strongly to the study of Judaism. He taught at the Advanced School for the Science of Judaism and wrote his late principle work "The Religion of Reason Out of the Sources of Judaism." Cohen was buried at the Schönhauser Allee cemetery. (Pisarek Photo Archive, c. 1915)

Feier der jüdischen Teilnehmer am Ersten Weltkrieg zu Weihnachten 1915 im Ausflugslokal Schlesinger im Grunewald. Die Weihnachtsfeier wurde in vielen assimilierten jüdischen Familien gefeiert. Wegen der zeitlichen Nähe zum jüdischen Chanukkafest sprach man dann auch gerne von »Weihnukka«. (M. Hampel)

Jewish soldiers in World War I celebrating Christmas in the Schlesinger restaurant in Grunewald in 1915. Many assimilated Jewish families celebrated Christmas. Because Christmas always fell around the same time as the Jewish holiday "Chanukah," it was often referred to as "Chrismukkah." (M. Hampel)

Hans Loevinson, aus der Familie Meyer-Loevinson stammend, als Armee-Krankenpfleger. Weitere biographische Angaben sind nicht bekannt. Deutsche Juden waren wie die Mehrheit der Bevölkerung zu Beginn des Ersten Weltkrieges sehr patriotisch eingestellt, und viele meldeten sich begeistert als Freiwillige. (Atelier Wertheim, Oktober 1914)

Hans Loevinson, from the Meyer-Loevinson family, seen here as an army orderly. No other information about him is known. German Jews, like the majority of Germans, were very patriotic when the First World War broke out and many enthusiastically volunteered for the army. (Atelier Wertheim, October 1914)

Der heute noch erhaltene Seitenflügel der Synagoge Kottbusser Ufer 48-50 (heute Fraenkelufer 10, Kreuzberg). Der Gemeindebaumeister Alexander Beer entwarf eine dreischiffige Basilika im neoklassizistischen Stil mit zweitausend Sitzplätzen, die 1916 eingeweiht wurde. Das in der Pogromnacht von 1938 ausgebrannte und im Zweiten Weltkrieg zerstörte Hauptgebäude wurde 1958/59 abgerissen. (Bildarchiv Pisarek, 1930)

The side wing of the synagogue at Kottbusser Ufer 48-50 (today's Fraenkelufer 10, Kreuzberg), which still exists today. The synagogue, designed by the community's house architect Alexander Beer as a neo-Classical three-naved basilica with seating for 2000, was dedicated in 1916. The main building, burned out in the 1938 pogrom and destroyed in World War II, was torn down in 1958/59. (Pisarek Photo Archive, 1930)

Innenansicht der Wochentags- und Jugendsynagoge Kottbusser Ufer 48-50, die im Seitenflügel untergebracht war. Seit dem Abriss des zerstörten Hauptgebäudes der Synagoge finden hier die Schabbatgottesdienste nach konservativem Ritus statt. (Bildarchiv Pisarek, um 1930)

View inside the weekday and youth synagogue at Kottbusser Ufer 48-50 that was housed in the side wing. Conservative Sabbath prayer services have been conducted here ever since the synagogue's main building was torn down. (Pisarek Photo Archive, c. 1930)

Max Karfunkel mit seinen acht Söhnen in Uniform während des Ersten Weltkrieges. Über 12 000 jüdische Soldaten kamen im Ersten Weltkrieg ums Leben. Ende 1916 wurde den antisemitischen Forderungen nachgegeben und die sogenannte Judenzählung durchgeführt, um die Kriegsbeteiligung jüdischer Soldaten zu untersuchen. Das Ergebnis der Zählung, die eine überdurchschnittliche Beteiligung von Juden ergab, wurde allerdings nicht veröffentlicht. (Kopie eines Photos)

Max Karfunkel with his eight sons in uniform during the First World War. More than 12,000 Jewish soldiers died during World War I. In response to anti-Semitic demands, a "Jewish census" was conducted at the end of 1916 to determine the number of Jewish soldiers involved in the war. The census found that given their percentage within the larger population, Jews were over-proportionately represented in the military, but the results were never published. (Copy of photo)

Die Geschwister Israel, Adolf Abraham und Salomon Weinberger während des Ersten Weltkrieges. Die drei Brüder betrieben zusammen mit einem weiteren Bruder und der Schwester eine Lebensmittelgroßhandlung in der Brunnenstraße 188-190 (Mitte). Die Firma wurde 1936 »arisiert«, und die Geschwister emigrierten in die USA und nach Palästina. (Albert Wegner)

The three siblings Israel, Adolf Abraham and Salomon Weinberger during the First World War. The three brothers and another brother and sister ran a wholesale grocery store at Brunnenstrasse 188-190 in Mitte. The business was "aryanized" by the National Socialists in 1936 and the siblings immigrated to the United States and Palestine. (Albert Wegner)

Rabbiner Benno Gottschalk mit jüdischen Verbindungsstudenten auf dem Jüdischen Friedhof Weißensee. Der 1883 in Berlin geborene Gottschalk war von 1933 bis 1939 Gemeinderabbiner am Tempel der Reformgemeinde in der Johannisstraße 16. Er konnte dann in die USA emigrieren und verstarb im Jahre 1966 in Los Angeles. (Ca. 1915)

Rabbi Benno Gottschalk with Jewish fraternity students at the Jewish cemetery in Weissensee. Gottschalk, born in 1883 in Berlin, was the community rabbi at the Reform Congregation Temple at Johannisstrasse 16 from 1933 to 1939. He was able to immigrate to the United States and died in Los Angeles in 1966. (c. 1915)

Ernst Emanuel Simon war Läufer im Bar Kochba Berlin, brandenburgischer Meister im 800-Meter-Lauf 1918 und 1919 sowie bayerischer Meister 1921. Nach seiner Einwanderung in Palästina 1924 arbeitete er als Sportarzt und war später Leiter des Turn- und Sportwesens in Israel. (1919)

Ernst Emanuel Simon was a runner in the Bar Kochba Berlin sports club. He was Brandenburg champion in the 800-Meter-run in 1918 and 1919 and Bavarian champion in 1921. After immigrating to Palestine in 1924 he worked as a sports doctor and was later the director of gymnastics and athletics in Israel. (1919)

Walther Rathenau (1867–1922) übernahm nach dem Tode seines Vaters Emil Rathenau (1838–1915) die Leitung der AEG. Während er völlig säkularisiert und assimiliert lebte, bekannte er sich zugleich in seinen Schriften zu seiner jüdischen Identität. Nach leitenden Ämtern im Ersten Weltkrieg war er 1919 an den Reparationsverhandlungen mit den Siegermächten beteiligt, worauf er von antisemitischen und deutschnationalen Kräften heftig angefeindet wurde. Er war ab 1921 erst Wiederaufbau- und kurz darauf Außenminister der Weimarer Republik. (1920)

After Emil Rathenau (1838–1915) died, his son Walther Rathenau (1867–1922) took over the AEG. Although he was a secular and assimilated German Jew, he acknowledged his Jewish identity in his writings. He held high-level leadership positions during War World I and was involved in the reparations negotiations with the victorious powers in 1919, causing anti-Semitic and German nationalistic forces to be hostile towards him. In 1921 he was appointed Reconstruction Minister and shortly thereafter Foreign Minister of the Weimar Republic. (1920)

Reichsaußenminister Walther Rathenau auf der Fahrt zur Konferenz nach Genua, Mai 1922. Er wurde am 24. Juni 1922 in seinem Auto – auf dem Wege von seiner Villa in der Koenigsallee 65 zum Außenministerium – an der Ecke Koenigsallee / Erdener Straße von rechtsradikalen Korpsoffizieren erschossen. Sein Grab befindet sich auf dem Städtischen Waldfriedhof Oberschöneweide.

Reich Foreign Minister Walther Rathenau traveling to a conference in Genoa in May 1922. On June 24, 1922, on his way by car from his villa at Koenigsallee 65 to the Foreign Office, he was shot and killed by rightwing corps officers at the corner of Koenigsallee and Erdener Strasse. His grave is located at the Städtischer Waldfriedhof cemetery in Oberschöneweide.

Rabbiner Meier Hildesheimer (1864–1934) war Leiter des Schulwerkes von Adass Jisroel und geschäftsführender Kurator des orthodoxen Rabbinerseminars, das sein Vater Esriel Hildesheimer gegründet hatte. Er liegt auf dem Friedhof von Adass Jisroel in Weißensee begraben. (Bildarchiv Pisarek, 1921)

Rabbi Meier Hildesheimer (1864–1934) was head of the Adass Yisroel School and directing curator of the orthodox rabbinical seminary founded by his father Esriel Hildesheimer. He is buried at the cemetery of Adass Yisroel in Weissensee. (Pisarek Photo Archive, 1921)

»Haus Vaterland« am Potsdamer Platz, Ecke Königgrätzer Straße. Seit 1928 war hier die bekannteste Adresse der Kempinski-Betriebe, die besonders bei Touristen sehr beliebt war. Auf mehreren Etagen befanden sich verschiedene nationale Spezialitätenrestaurants und ein Tanzcafé. Das kriegszerstörte Gebäude wurde 1974 abgerissen. (Photopostkarte, um 1929)

"Haus Vaterland" at Potsdamer Platz, on the corner of Königgrätzer Strasse. By 1928 this was the best known of all the Kempinski business, especially popular among tourists. Various restaurants served national specialties on different levels and there was also a dance café. The war-damaged building was torn down in 1974. (Postcard photo, c. 1929)

Gerhart Friedmann

Mitglieder der Ruderabteilung des Vereins Jüdischer Studenten. Die Abteilung wurde 1907 gegründet und hatte in Niederschöneweide ihren Treffpunkt. Rudern galt den Zionisten als »ideale Leibesübung« sowie »hochdisziplinierter Mannschaftssport« und ermöglichte »gemeinsame Naturerlebnisse«. Nach der zwangsweisen Auflösung des Rudervereins im Jahre 1933 wurden die Boote nach Palästina überführt, um dort diesen Sport zu etablieren. (Ostern 1919)

Members of the rowing division of the Jewish student Association. This division, founded in 1907, had its meeting place in Niederschöneweide. Rowing was regarded by Zionists as "ideal physical exercise" and a "highly disciplined team sport" that made it possible to "experience nature together." After the rowing association was forced to close down in 1933, the boats were brought to Palestine to establish the sport there. (Easter 1919)

Gerhard Friedmann in der Uniform einer schlagenden jüdischen Studentenverbindung. Über ihn sind leider keine weiteren biographischen Angaben verfügbar. (Weihnachten 1923)

Gerhard Friedmann in the uniform of the Jewish student fencing association. Unfortunately, nothing more is known about him. (Christmas 1923)

Aus dem Photoalbum von Heinz Gottschalk: Der Bund Jüdischer Pfadfinder, Pfingstlager 1928 des 4., 7. und 11. Zuges Berlin, Stettin und Hamburg am Großen Drewensee. Gottschalk wurde 1902 in Berlin geboren. Nach der Schule begann er eine Ausbildung als Apotheker. In seiner Freizeit war er seit 1916 Mitglied des zionistischen Jugendbundes Blau-Weiß und seit 1925 Mitglied des Bundes Jüdischer Pfadfinder. Mit Blau-Weiß unternahm er eine Vielzahl von Fahrten, so auch 1925 nach Palästina.

From Heinz Gottschalk's photo album: The Jewish Boy Scouts of the 4th, 7th and 11th divisions, Berlin, Stettin and Hamburg, at Grosser Drewensee, Whitsun camp, 1928. Gottschalk was born in Berlin in 1902. After finishing school he began an apprenticeship as a pharmacist. He became a member of the Zionist Blue White Youth Alliance in 1916 and joined the Jewish Boy Scouts in 1925. He took a number of trips with Blue White including one to Palestine in 1925.

Aus dem Photoalbum von Heinz Gottschalk: Der jüdische Pfadfinderbund während eines Ausflugs zum Seddiner See am 2. Mai 1926. Infolge der Krankheit seines Vaters übernahm Gottschalk 1925 das Familienunternehmen, eine Möbelagentur. 1933 emigrierte er nach Palästina, wo das frischverheiratete Ehepaar Heinz und Liselotte Gottschalk in der neugegründeten Siedlung Ramot Hashawim arbeitete. 1945 gelang es Heinz Gottschalk, eine eigene Apotheke zu eröffnen. Er starb 1987.

From Heinz Gottschalk's photo album: The Jewish Boy Scouts during a trip to the Seddiner Lake on May 2, 1926. After his father fell ill, Gottschalk took over the family furniture business in 1925. He immigrated to Palestine in 1933 where the recently married couple Heinz und Liselotte Gottschalk worked in the newly established settlement called Ramot Hashawim. In 1945 Heinz Gottschalk was able to open his own pharmacy. He died in 1987.

Aus dem Photoalbum von Heinz Gottschalk: Die Purimfeier des 9. Zuges des Bundes Jüdischer Pfadfinder im Jahre 1926. Das Purimfest erinnert an die Rettung vor der geplanten Vernichtung des jüdischen Volkes, wie sie im biblischen Buch Ester erzählt wird.

From Heinz Gottschalk's photo album: The 9th division of the Jewish Boy Scouts celebrating Purim in 1926. The holiday of Purim recalls the story recounted in the Book of Esther about how the Jewish people were saved from extermination.

Koschere Konditorei und Café Krakauer von David Kempler (1888–1954) in der Grenadierstraße 20-21 (heute Almstadtstraße, Mitte) im Scheunenviertel. Von rechts: seine Töchter Fanny und Miri, seine Frau Liebe (1888–1974) und im Wagen sein jüngster Sohn Hillel. Die Familie emigrierte nach der nationalsozialistischen Machtübernahme 1933 nach Palästina und lebte in Tel Aviv. (Ca. 1926)

Jewish Pastry shop and Café Krakauer run by David Kempler (1888–1954) at Grenadierstrasse 20-21 (today's Almstadtstrasse, Mitte) in the Scheunenviertel. From the right: his daughters Fanny and Miri, his wife Liebe (1888–1974) and his youngest son Hillel in the baby carriage. The family immigrated to Palestine after the National Socialists took power in 1933 and lived in Tel Aviv. (c. 1926)

Familienbild von Jakob Reiss (ganz
rechts) mit seinen Eltern und fünf
Geschwistern. Reiss wurde 1908 in
Polen geboren und zog mit seiner
Familie 1914 nach Berlin. Er besuch-
te die Knabenschule der Jüdischen
Gemeinde in der Großen Hambur-
ger Straße und engagierte sich in
der orthodox-zionistischen Jugend-
bewegung. Im Jahre 1935 emigrierte
er gemeinsam mit seinen Eltern und
der jüngsten Schwester nach Paläs-
tina, wo bereits die anderen Ge-
schwister lebten. Reiss starb 1985 in
Jerusalem. (Rudolf Nase, ca. 1920)

*Family photo taken of Jakob
Reiss (far right) with his parents
and five siblings. Reiss was born
in Poland in 1908 and moved
with his family to Berlin in 1914.
He attended the Jewish Commu-
nity Boys School on Grosse
Hamburger Strasse and was
active in the Orthodox-Zionist
youth movement. He immigrated
with his parents and youngest
sister to Palestine in 1935 where the
other siblings were already settled.
Reiss died in 1985 in Jerusalem.
(Rudolf Nase, c. 1920)*

Im Gemeindehaus der Jüdischen Gemeinde in der Oranienburger Straße 28 waren Büros wie Gemeinde-, Schul- und Finanzverwaltung untergebracht. Außerdem befindet sich bis heute auch das Gesamtarchiv der Deutschen Juden in diesem Gebäude. (Herbert Seeliger, um 1930)

A number of offices including the community, school and finance administration were housed in the Jewish community center at Oranienburger Strasse 28 (Mitte). The Complete Archive of German Jewry is still held in this building. (Herbert Seeliger, c. 1930)

Der Israelitisch-Sephardische Verein zu Berlin wurde 1905 gegründet. Um 1930 zählte er fünfhundert Mitglieder, die überwiegend aus dem Osmanischen Reich waren. Der Verein mietete eine größere Wohnung in der Lützowstraße 111 (Tiergarten) und richtete darin seine Synagoge ein. (Abraham Pisarek, um 1930)

The Israeli-Sephardic Association of Berlin was founded in 1905. It had about five hundred members by the end of the 1920s, mostly from the Ottoman Empire. The association rented a large apartment at Lützowstrasse 111 (Tiergarten) and established its synagogue there. (Abraham Pisarek, c. 1930)

In der sephardischen Privatsynagoge Lützowstraße 111 ausgestellte Kultgegenstände wie Chanukkaleuchter, Schabbatleuchter, Vorhang für den Toraschrein, Sederteller für Pessach. (Abraham Pisarek, um 1930)

Religious objects displayed in the private Sephardic synagogue at Lützowstrasse 111: Chanukah menorahs, Sabbath candle holder, curtain for the Torah ark, Seder plate for Passover. (Abraham Pisarek, c. 1930)

תורת ה' תמימה
כ ת
נדבת
ר' ברוך חיים
בן מרדכי נ"י
ואשתו רחל
בת שבתי
קוגעלמאַנן

Sephardische Juden beim Teppichknüpfen. Die Nachfahren der aus Spanien vertriebenen Juden siedelten sich vor allem im östlichen Mittelmeerraum und in den Niederlanden an. Von dort kamen sie auch nach Deutschland und brachten ihre eigenen Traditionen, Riten und Fertigkeiten mit. (Bildarchiv Pisarek, 1932)

Sephardic Jews beating a carpet. Most of the descendents of the Jews who were expelled from Spain settled either in the eastern Mediterranean region or in the Netherlands. They later moved from there to Germany and brought their traditions, rituals and skills with them. (Pisarek Photo Archive, 1932)

Der Photograph Abraham Pisarek wurde 1901 in Przedbórz (Polen) geboren und wanderte 1919 nach Deutschland ein. Er lebte von 1924 bis 1928 in Palästina, kehrte aber enttäuscht nach Berlin zurück. Er stand der KPD nahe und engagierte sich in der Arbeiterphotographie. Ihm sind unzählige Photos vom jüdischen Leben in Berlin zu verdanken, besonders aus der Zeit zwischen 1933 bis 1945, die er durch eine Reihe von Umständen überlebte. Er starb 1983 in West-Berlin. (Bildarchiv Pisarek, um 1928)

The photographer Abraham Pisarek was born in Przedbórz (Poland) in 1901 and immigrated to Germany in 1919. He lived in Palestine from 1924 to 1928 but disappointed, returned to Berlin. He had close ties to the KPD (Communist Party) and actively photographed the working class. Thanks to him we have countless photos documenting Jewish life in Berlin, especially between 1933 and 1945. He survived these years through a series of fortunate circumstances and died in West Berlin in 1983. (Pisarek Photo Archive, c. 1928)

Kaffeerunde von Georg Tietz, Adolf und Robert Jandorf. Georg Tietz (1889–1953) war der Sohn von Oscar Tietz (1858–1923), der zusammen mit seinem Onkel Hermann Tietz (1837–1907) den Kaufhauskonzern begründet hatte. Er führte das Familienunternehmen gemeinsam mit seinem Bruder Martin und seinem Schwager Dr. Hugo Zwillenberg nicht nur fort, sondern erweiterte es 1926 durch den Kauf der Jandorf-Warenhäuser. (Satrapp)

Georg Tietz, Adolf and Robert Jandorf taking a coffee break. Georg Tietz (1889–1953) was the son of Oscar Tietz (1858–1923) who established the department store group with his uncle Hermann Tietz (1837–1907). He not only continued to head the family business together with his brother Martin and his brother-in-law Dr. Hugo Zwillenberg, but also expanded it in 1926 when he purchased the Jandorf stores. (Satrapp)

Das Warenhaus Tietz in der Leipziger Straße nach der Fertigstellung im Jahre 1900. Der Inhaber und Geschäftsführer Oscar Tietz begann mit Startkapital seines Onkels Hermann in Gera mit einem Weißwarengeschäft. Dem ersten Berliner Kaufhaus in der Leipziger Straße folgten weitere am Alexanderplatz und in der Frankfurter Allee. Nach der Übernahme des Jandorf-Konzerns im Jahre 1926 war das Familienunternehmen Tietz der größte Warenhauskonzern Europas.

The Tietz department store on Leipziger Strasse after its completion in 1900. Its owner and manager Oscar Tietz began with a linen business in Gera, using capital from his uncle Hermann. The first Berlin department store on Leipziger Strasse was followed by others on Alexanderplatz and Frankfurter Allee. After acquiring the Jandorf group in 1926, the Tietz business became the largest department store group in Europe.

TIETZ
TIETZ

Rudolf Mosse mit Freunden im Logenhaus Joachimstaler Straße 13 (Charlottenburg). Die jüdische Loge Bne Briss (»Söhne des Bundes«) hatte in diesem Gebäude ihren Berliner Hauptsitz. Die Loge wurde 1843 von deutsch-jüdischen Einwanderern in New York gegründet. Ein deutscher Ableger, die Deutsche Reichsloge Bne Briss, entstand 1882 in Berlin. Hauptaufgabe der Loge war (und ist bis heute) die Unterstützung sozialer Einrichtungen und karitative Hilfe. (Chanukka 1928)

Rudolf Mosse with friends in the lodge at Joachimstaler Strasse 13 (Charlottenburg). The Jewish lodge "Bne Briss" (Sons of the Covenant) had its Berlin headquarters in this building. The lodge was founded in 1843 by German-Jewish immigrants in New York. A German branch, the German Reich Lodge Bne Briss, was established in 1882 in Berlin. The main task of the lodge (still today) is to support social institutions and engage in charity work. (Chanukah 1928)

Der Verleger Samuel Fischer (1859–1934, Mitte) mit den Schriftstellern Thomas Mann (1875–1955, links) und Jakob Wassermann (1873–1934). Fischer kam 1881 nach Berlin und gründete hier fünf Jahre später den erfolgreichen S. Fischer Verlag, der neben Mann und Wassermann u.a. auch Gerhart Hauptmann, Franz Kafka, Stefan Zweig und Hermann Hesse verlegte. Er wohnte seit 1905 bis zu seinem Tod in einer Jugendstilvilla in der Erdener Straße 8. (Bildarchiv Pisarek, um 1930)

The publisher Samuel Fischer (1859–1934, middle) with the authors Thomas Mann (1875–1955, left) and Jakob Wassermann (1873–1934). Fischer came to Berlin in 1881 and five years later founded the successful S. Fischer Publishing House here. It published works by Mann and Wassermann as well as by Gerhart Hauptmann, Franz Kafka, Stefan Zweig and Hermann Hesse. He lived in an art nouveau villa at Erdener Strasse 8 from 1905 until his death. (Pisarek Photo Archive, c. 1930).

Die von Ehrenfried Hessel entworfene Synagoge in der Fasanenstraße 79/80 (Charlottenburg) wurde im Unterschied zu den bis dahin gebauten Hinterhofsynagogen selbstbewusst und repräsentativ freistehend errichtet. Sie wurde im Jahre 1912 eingeweiht, im Novemberpogrom 1938 in Brand gesteckt und dabei völlig zerstört. Nach dem Abriss der Ruine wurde hier 1959 das neue Jüdische Gemeindezentrum eingeweiht. (1930)

Unlike the back courtyard synagogues that had previously been erected, the synagogue at Fasanenstrasse 79/80 (Charlottenburg), designed by Ehrenfried Hessel, was an independent, representative structure evoking confidence. It was dedicated in 1912 and completely destroyed by a fire set to it during the November pogrom of 1938. After the ruins were torn down, a new Jewish community center was opened here in 1959. (1930)

Vor der Synagoge Fasanenstraße 79/80 nach einem Gottesdienst. Bis zu 1720 Besucher fanden in dem gewaltigen Bau unter drei Kuppeln Platz. Die Gottesdienste folgten dem liberalen Ritus. Das auf dem Foto zu sehende vorgesetzte Eingangsportal und ein Teil der Fassadenpilaster wurden für den Neubau des Jüdischen Gemeindezentrums 1959 am selben Ort wiederverwendet. (Hans G. Casparius, 1929)

In front of the synagogue at Fasanenstrasse 79/80 following prayer services. There was seating for up to 1720 visitors in the massive structure set beneath three domes. Services were conducted according to the liberal tradition. The entrance portal and a piece of the facade pilaster, visible in the photo, were re-integrated into the new Jewish community center building that was erected in 1959 at the same spot. (Hans G. Casparius, 1929)

יודישע און העברעאישע ליטעראטור
Jüd. Schallplatten
Antiquariat
ספרים
עתיקים

Orthodoxer Jude mit fünf Kindern in der Grenadierstraße. Im Scheunenviertel lebten vor allem die Armen, Zugewanderten, Ausgestoßenen und Gescheiterten. Viele vor den Pogromen in Russland, Litauen und Polen geflüchtete Juden siedelten sich hier an. Die neugierigen Blicke der Passanten zeigen, dass selbst hier orthodoxes Judentum nicht für alle selbstverständlich war. (Walter Gircke, 1928)

Orthodox Jew with his five children on Grenadierstrasse. Mostly poor people, immigrants, outcasts and failures lived in the Scheunenviertel. Many Jews fled pogroms in Russia, Lithuania and Poland and settled here. The curious glances of passersby suggest that for some orthodox Judaism was not commonplace, even here. (Walter Gircke, 1928)

Buch- und Schallplattenhandlung in der Grenadierstraße (heute Almstadtstraße, Mitte) im Scheunenviertel. Hier wurden »Jüdische Schallplatten« und (in hebräischen Lettern) »Jiddische und Hebräische Literatur« angeboten. Die hebräische Inschrift an der Wand lautet übersetzt: »Alte Bücher«. (Carl Weinrother, 1928)

Book and record store on Grenadierstrasse (today's Almstadtstrasse, Mitte) in the Scheunenviertel. The store sold "Jewish records" and "Yiddish and Hebrew literature" (in Hebrew letters). The Hebrew inscription on the wall says "Old Books" (Carl Weinrother, 1928)

Ephraimpalais an der Ecke Mühlendamm/Poststraße, benannt nach Veitel Heine Ephraim (1703–1775), der als Hofjuwelier, Bankier und Münzpächter vermögend wurde. Im Jahre 1762 kaufte Ephraim das Palais, das um 1700 für den Apotheker Karl Walter Tonnenbinder errichtet worden war, und ließ es im Rokokostil prächtig ausbauen. Das Palais wurde 1987, nachdem die Fassadensteine nach dem Abriss über fünfzig Jahre lang eingelagert waren, in unmittelbarer Nähe wiederaufgebaut. (Bildarchiv Pisarek, um 1930)

Ephraim Palace at the corner of Mühlendamm and Poststrasse was named after Veitel Heine Ephraim (1703–1775), who made his fortune as a court jeweler, banker and mint master. In 1762 Ephraim bought the palace that had originally been built for the pharmacist Karl Walter Tonnenbinder around 1700. Ephraim had it converted magnificently into the Rococo style. When the building was torn down, the facade stones were stored away. Fifty years later, in 1987, the palace was reconstructed very close to the original site. (Pisarek Photo Archive, c.1930)

Der Journalist und Schriftsteller Theodor Wolff (1868–1943) war seit 1894 Pariser Korrespondent für das »Berliner Tageblatt« und ab 1906 dessen Chefredakteur. In seinem Leitartikel nach der Machtübernahme der Nationalsozialisten rief er zum Widerstand auf. Nach dem Reichstagsbrand flüchtete er nach Frankreich, wo er zehn Jahre später von der Gestapo verhaftet wurde. Nachdem er mehrere Gefängnisse und das KZ Sachsenhausen durchlitten hatte, starb er im Jüdischen Krankenhaus in Wedding. (1918)

The journalist and author Theodor Wolff (1868–1943) had been the Paris correspondent for the "Berliner Tageblatt" since 1894 and became its editor in chief in 1906. He called for resistance in an editorial he wrote after the National Socialists took power. After the Reichstag was set on fire he fled to France where he was arrested by the Gestapo ten years later. Having suffered through different prisons and in the Sachsenhausen concentration camp, he died in the Jewish hospital in Wedding. (1918)

Das Ehepaar Max und Martha Liebermann in seiner Wohnung am Pariser Platz 7. Der Maler Max Liebermann (1847–1935) wurde 1933 von den Nationalsozialisten aus allen Ämtern vertrieben, seine Werke wurden aus den Museen entfernt. Gesellschaftlich isoliert, starb er 1935 und wurde auf dem Jüdischen Friedhof Schönhauser Allee begraben. Seine Witwe Martha wählte hochbetagt kurz vor der geplanten Deportation im Jahre 1943 den Freitod. (Felix H. Man, 1930)

The married couple Max and Martha Liebermann in their apartment at Pariser Platz 7. The National Socialists forced the painter Max Liebermann (1847–1935) to resign from his positions in 1933 and his works were removed from museums. Socially isolated, he died in 1935 and was buried at the Jewish cemetery at Schönhauser Allee. His widow, Martha, well advanced in years, committed suicide in 1943, shortly before her approaching deportation. (Felix H. Man, 1930)

Verleihung der Preußischen Staatsmedaille an Max Liebermann (sitzend, Zweiter von links) an seinem 80. Geburtstag 1927. Stehend der preußische Kultusminister Carl Heinrich Becker. Liebermann war Gründungsmitglied der Berliner Secession und ab 1920 Präsident der Preußischen Akademie der Künste. Er sagte einmal: »Ich hatte zu viele Feinde. Ich bot ja auch drei Angriffsflächen: Ich war erstens Jude, zweitens reich und drittens hatte ich Talent. Eines davon hätte doch genügt.«

Max Lieberman (seated second from the left) receiving the Prussian National Medal on his 80th birthday in 1927. The Prussian Minister of Culture Carl Heinrich Becker is standing. Liebermann was a founding member of the Berlin Secession und was appointed president of the Prussian Academy of Arts in 1920. He once said: "I had too many enemies. I offered them three targets: First I was a Jew, second I was rich, and third I was talented. One of these would have sufficed."

Das jüdische Buch- und Schreibwarengeschäft von Hirsch Lewin in der Grenadierstraße 28 im Scheunenviertel. In dem Laden wurden auch hebräische Bücher, jüdische Traditionsliteratur, Stickereien für den Synagogalgebrauch (z.B. Gebetsschals, Kippas, Gebetbuch-Etuis) und jüdische Schallplatten angeboten. (Um 1930)

Hirsch Lewin's Jewish book and stationary store on Grenadierstrasse 28 in the Scheunenviertel. The store also sold Hebrew books, traditional Jewish literature, embroidery for use in the synagogue (for prayer shawls, yamulkas and prayer book covers) and Jewish records. (c. 1930)

Zwei orthodoxe Juden in Berlin. Einer trägt einen Palmzweig (»Lulaw«), der für das siebentägige Laubhüttenfest Sukkot benötigt wird, das jeweils im Herbst, fünfzehn Tage nach dem jüdischen Neujahrsfest, gefeiert wird. Zur Erinnerung an den Auszug aus Ägypten wird eine Laubhütte auf dem Balkon, im Hinterhof oder im Garten errichtet, in der möglichst viel Zeit betend und lesend verbracht wird. (Oskar Marcus, 1932)

Two Orthodox Jews in Berlin. One is wearing a palm branch (Lulaw), used in the celebration of Sukhot, the Feast of Tabernacles. This seven-day holiday is celebrated in the fall, fifteen days after the Jewish new year. In memory of the Jews' departure from Egypt, a temporary hut for praying and reading is built on a balcony or in a back courtyard or garden. (Oskar Marcus, 1932)

Die aus England stammende Lily Montagu (1873–1963) predigt in der Synagoge der Reformgemeinde in der Johannisstraße 16. Sie war eine Mitbegründerin der National Organization of Girl's Clubs und der Union of Progressive Judaism. (Bildarchiv Pisarek, 1928)

Lily Montagu (1873–1963), from England, preached in the synagogue of the Reform Congregation at Johannisstrasse 16. She was co-founder of the National Organization of Girl's Clubs and the Union of Progressive Judaism. (Pisarek Photo Archive, 1928)

Der jüdische Kantor Towje Hakonen wurde in Äthiopien als ein Angehöriger des jüdischen Volkes des Beta Israel geboren und lebte in New York. Auf einer Konzertreise war er auch zu Gast in der Singakademie Berlin. (Bildarchiv Pisarek, um 1930)

The Jewish cantor Towje Hakonen was born in Ethiopia as a member of the Jewish people of Beta Israel and lived in New York. During a concert tour he was invited to the Singing Academy in Berlin. (Pisarek Photo Archive, c. 1930)

Die Jüdische Kleinkunstbühne Kaftan in der Jägerstraße (Mitte). Die Schauspieler Ruth Klinger (1906 Prag – 1989 Haifa) und ihr Ehemann Maxim Sakaschansky gründeten 1930 dieses Theater, das ausschließlich jüdische Stücke aufführte und beim Publikum sehr beliebt war. Bereits 1933 gelang ihnen die Emigration nach Palästina. Die Buchstaben des Namens »Kaftan« sollen hebräische Lettern imitieren. (Bildarchiv Pisarek, 1930/31)

The Jewish cabaret "Kaftan" on Jägerstrasse (Mitte). The actors Ruth Klinger (1906 Prague – 1989 Haifa) and her husband Maxim Sakaschansky founded this theater in 1930 and only Jewish works were performed here. The theater was very popular with the public. The couple managed to immigrate to Palestine as early as 1933. The letters of the name "Kaftan" are intended to imitate Hebrew lettering. (Pisarek Photo Archive, 1930/31)

Ernst Deutsch (1890–1969) in der Hauptrolle des »Jud Süß« von Paul Kornfeld (1889–1942 Ghetto Lodz), Uraufführung am 7. Oktober 1930 im Theater am Schiffbauerdamm (Regie Leopold Jessner, Bühnenbild Caspar Neher), hier in einer Szene mit Otto Wernicke (links) und Erich Ponto (rechts). In der NS-Zeit emigrierte Deutsch über England in die USA und nach Argentinien. Im Jahre 1947 kehrte er nach Berlin zurück. Sein Grab befindet sich auf dem Jüdischen Friedhof Heerstraße.

Ernst Deutsch (1890–1969) in the main role of a play by Paul Kornfeld (1889–1942 Lodz Ghetto) titled "Jud Süss" (The Jew Suess), here in a scene with Otto Wernicke (right) and Erich Ponto (left). It premiered on October 7, 1930 in Theater am Schiffbauerdamm (director Leopold Jessner, stage design Caspar Neher). Deutsch immigrated to the United States via England during the Nazi era and later settled in Argentina. He returned to Berlin in 1947. He is buried at the Jewish cemetery on Heerstrasse.

Goldene Hochzeit des Ehepaars Heinrich und Helene Valentin in Berlin. Typisches Beispiel für eine assimilierte jüdische Familie, die sich äußerlich in keiner Weise von ihrer nichtjüdischen Umwelt unterschied. (1921)

Heinrich and Helene Valentin celebrating their golden wedding anniversary in Berlin. They are a typical example of an assimilated Jewish family whose appearance in no way distinguishes them from the non-Jewish world in which they live. (1921)

Gesellschaftstee anläßlich der Gründung der Jüdischen Altershilfe im Jahre 1931. Durch die Inflation gingen viele Vermögen verloren, und unzählige Juden waren deshalb im Alter hilfsbedürftig. Die Gemeinde und private Initiativen versuchten auch durch Benefizveranstaltungen, neue Altersheime zu finanzieren, und sammelten Sachspenden. (Bildarchiv Pisarek).

Society tea in honor of the Jewish charity organization for the aged that opened in 1931. Many fortunes were lost due to inflation and many elderly Jews were consequently dependent on charity. The Jewish community and many private initiatives organized benefit events to raise money and finance new homes for the aged. (Pisarek Photo Archive).

Albert Einstein (1879–1955) mit Geige in der Neuen Synagoge in der Oranienburger Straße 30 bei einem Wohltätigkeitskonzert am 29. Januar 1930. Einstein spielte – zusammen mit Alfred Lewandowski an der Violine und begleitet von Arthur Zepke an der Orgel – das Adagio aus dem Doppelkonzert C-Moll von J.S. Bach. Alfred Lewandowski war der Sohn von Louis Lewandowski, dem Begründer der modernen Synagogalmusik. (Erich Salomon)

Albert Einstein (1879–1955) with a violin in the New Synagogue at Oranienburger Strasse 30 during a benefit concert on January 29, 1930. Einstein, accompanied by Alfred Lewandowski on the violin and Arthur Zepke on the organ, played the Adagio from J.S. Bach's double concerto in C minor. Alfred Lewandowski was the son of Louis Lewandowski, the founder of modern synagogue music. (Erich Salomon)

Albert Einstein und seine Privatsekretärin Helen Dukas während desselben Wohltätigkeitskonzerts für das Wohlfahrts- und Jugendamt der Jüdischen Gemeinde Berlin. Der Physiker und Nobelpreisträger Einstein war streitbarer Pazifist, bewusster Jude und engagierter Zionist. (Erich Salomon)

Albert Einstein and his private secretary Helen Dukas during the same benefit concert for the charity and youth office of the Berlin Jewish community. The physicist and Nobel Prize winner Einstein was a militant pacifist and active Zionist. (Erich Salomon)

Professor Ismar Elbogen und Studenten der Hochschule für die Wissenschaft des Judentums im Jahre 1932. Der Historiker Elbogen (1874–1943) war einer von fünf hauptamtlichen Dozenten an der Hochschule für die Wissenschaft des Judentums. Sein bis heute nachgedrucktes Hauptwerk ist »Der jüdische Gottesdienst in seiner geschichtlichen Entwicklung« von 1913. Er konnte in die USA emigrieren und starb in New York.

Professor Ismar Elbogen and students of the Advanced School for the Science of Judaism in 1932. The historian Elbogen (1874–1943) was one of five full-time lecturers at the Advanced School for the Science of Judaism. His most important work, published in 1913 and still in print today is titled "Jewish Liturgy. A Comprehensive History." He was able to immigrate to the United States and died in New York.

Schüler der Waldschule Kaliski vor dem Sportclub Charlottenburg im Eichkamp, wo die Schule in einigen Räumen untergebracht war. Die in Breslau geborene Pädagogin Lotte Kaliski (1908–1995) ging nach ihrem Staatsexamen nach Berlin und gründete diese private jüdische Schule 1932 als Tagesinternat. Sie emigrierte 1938 in die USA, wo sie wieder eine Schule, nun für lernbehinderte Kinder, gründete. (1932/33)

Schoolchildren of the Waldschule Kaliski in front of the sports club Charlottenburg in Eichkamp, where the school was located in a few rooms. The educator Lotte Kaliski (1908–1995) was born in Breslau and moved to Berlin after completing her state examination. She founded this private Jewish day school there in 1932. She immigrated to the United States in 1938 and founded another school there for children with learning disabilities. (1932/33)

Der im Jahre 1922 gegründete Preußische Landesverband Jüdischer Gemeinden bei seiner Jubiläumsfeier zum zehnjährigen Bestehen. Zweiter von rechts ist der Rechtsanwalt und zionistische Politiker Dr. Alfred Klee (1875 Berlin – 1943 KZ Westerbork), der seit 1920 im Vorstand der Jüdischen Gemeinde Berlin und seit 1925 Vizepräsident im Preußischen Landesverband war. (Abraham Pisarek, 1932)

The Prussian National Association of Jewish Communities, founded in 1922, celebrated its tenth anniversary. Dr. Alfred Klee (1875 Berlin – 1943 Westerbork concentration camp), second from the right, was an attorney and Zionist politician who had served on the board of the Berlin Jewish Community since 1920 and was vice president of the Prussian National Association since 1925. (Abraham Pisarek, 1932)

Tagung des Preußischen Landesverbandes Jüdischer Gemeinden im Preußischen Herrenhaus in Berlin 1932. Nachdem in der Weimarer Republik die Bildung einer Gesamtdachorganisation nicht durchführbar war, schlossen sich die jüdischen Gemeinden in Landesverbänden zusammen, um so als öffentlich-rechtliche Körperschaften anerkannt zu werden. Dem Preußischen Landesverband, der zwei Drittel aller deutschen Juden repräsentierte, blieb diese Anerkennung durch die Ministerialbürokratie jedoch versagt.

Conference of the Prussian National Association of Jewish Communities in the Prussian House of Lords in Berlin in 1932. After efforts to establish an umbrella organization failed in the Weimar Republic, the Jewish communities joined into state associations as a way to gain status as an institution under public law. The Prussian National Association, which represented two-thirds of all Jews in Germany, was nonetheless denied this status by the Prussian ministerial administration.

Der Jüdische Turn- und Sportverein Bar Kochba beim Propagandalauf Jüdischer Sportvereine 1927. Berlin war neben Wien das Zentrum des zionistischen Sportlebens. Hier wurden nicht nur körperliche Ertüchtigung und Wehrsport getrieben, sondern auch die hebräische Sprachausbildung und neue Turnkommandos gefördert. (G. Riebicke)

Bar Kochba, the Jewish gymnastics and sports club during the propaganda race held by the Jewish sports clubs of Berlin in 1927. Berlin and Vienna were the center of Zionist athletics. Along with physical training and defense sports, these clubs also taught Hebrew and encouraged the development of new gymnastic drills. (G. Riebicke)

Chanukkafeier im Jüdischen Jugendwohn- und Lehrlingsheim in der Mühlenstraße 20 (heute 24) in Berlin-Pankow. Das Lichterfest Chanukka fällt ungefähr in die Weihnachtszeit und erinnert an das Ölwunder in der Makkabäer-Zeit, als ein einziger Krug Öl acht Tage – anstatt einen Tag – ausreichte. (Ca. 1931)

Chanukah party in the Jewish youth and apprentice home at Mühlenstrasse 20 (today no. 24) in Berlin-Pankow. The Chanukah festival of light falls around the same time as Christmas and recalls the miracle during the age of the Maccabees when a single jug of oil, enough for a single day, lasted an entire eight days. (c. 1931)

Schulorchester des Jüdischen Jugendwohn- und Lehrlingsheims Berlin-Pankow. Dieses Heim wurde 1896 durch den Verein zur Förderung des Handwerks unter den Juden eingeweiht und bot bis zu sechzig Jugendlichen Unterkunft und Ausbildung. (Ca. 1931)

School orchestra of the Jewish youth and apprentice home in Berlin-Pankow. This home was opened in 1896 by the Association to Support Jewish Artisans and provided housing and schooling to sixty youths. (c. 1931)

Schusterei des Jüdischen Jugend-wohn- und Lehrlingsheims. In den hauseigenen Werkstätten auf dem Hinterhof gab es außerdem auch noch eine Möbeltischlerei. Von der Ausbildung in Handwerksberufen versprach man sich bessere Berufschancen nicht nur in Deutschland, sondern auch in Palästina. (Ca. 1931)

Shoemaker of the Jewish youth and apprentice home. There was also a cabinetmaker among the workshops located in the back courtyard of the home. The young people hoped that learning an artisan trade would provide them with better work opportunities in Germany, but also in Palestine. (c. 1931)

Die Synagoge Prinzregentenstraße 69/70 (Wilmersdorf) wurde am 16. September 1930 als letzte Gemeindesynagoge in Berlin vor der nationalsozialistischen Machtübernahme mit einem feierlichen Gottesdienst eingeweiht. Rabbiner Leo Baeck hielt die Festpredigt. Das Photo zeigt im Hintergrund – typisch für Gottesdienste nach liberalem Ritus – Vorlesepult, Toraschrein und darüber die Orgel. (Abraham Pisarek)

The synagogue at Prinzregentenstrasse 69/70 (Wilmersdorf) was dedicated with a ceremonial prayer service on September 16, 1930. It was the last community synagogue to open before the National Socialists took power. The sermon was given by Rabbi Leo Baeck. The bima and the Torah ark with the organ above it – typical of liberal prayer services – can be seen in the back of the photo. (Abraham Pisarek)

Der gewaltige Kuppelrundbau der Synagoge Prinzregentenstraße 69/70 bot 2300 Besuchern Platz. Die Synagoge wurde in der Pogromnacht von 1938 durch Brandstiftung zerstört. Der Gemeindebaumeister Alexander Beer (1873–1943), der diese Synagoge entworfen hatte und nach ihrer Zerstörung den Abriss verfügen musste, wurde im KZ Theresienstadt ermordet. (Photopostkarte, Bildarchiv Pisarek, um 1930)

The powerful domed circular architecture of the synagogue at Prinzregentenstrasse 69/70 provided seating to 2300 worshippers. The synagogue was destroyed by a fire set during the pogrom of 1938. The community's architect Alexander Beer (1873–1943), who designed this synagogue and who had to oversee its demolition after it was destroyed, was murdered in the Theresienstadt concentration camp. (Photo postcard, Pisarek Photo Archive, c. 1930)

Aufmarsch einer Frauengruppe des Bar Kochba Berlin. Im Jahre 1910 hat sich durch Abspaltung vom Jüdischen Turnverein Bar Kochba der Jüdische Frauenbund für Turnen und Sport gegründet, um für die Emanzipation der Frauen einzutreten. Ende der 1920er Jahre scheint es wieder eine Annäherung an Bar Kochba gegeben zu haben. (1930er Jahre)

A women's group of Bar Kochba Berlin marching. In 1910 the Bar Kochba split and the Jewish Women's Association for Gymnastics and Sports was founded to work more strongly for the emancipation of women. It appears that by the end of the 1920s the women's association had re-established closer ties to Bar Kochba. (1930s)

Gymnastikgruppe des Bar Kochba Berlin beim Training. Olga Löbel-Glücklich (rechts stehend) wurde 1905 in Berlin geboren. Mitte der 1920er Jahre trat sie in den Verein ein, betrieb dort Tanz- und Sportgymnastik und wurde selbst Gymnastiklehrerin. 1938 wanderte sie mit ihrem späteren Ehemann Hermann Bischoff nach Südrhodesien aus. (Ca. 1930)

Gymnastics group of the Jewish gymnastics and sports club Bar Kochba Berlin during training. Olga Löbel-Glücklich (standing at the right) was born in Berlin in 1905. She joined the club in the mid-1920s, running dance and sports gymnastics and became a gymnastics teacher herself. She immigrated to southern Rhodesia with her future husband Hermann Bischoff in 1938. (c. 1930)

Alt-Berliner Schmuckaufsätze für Torarollen und ein Beschneidungsstuhl aus Märkisch-Friedland im Jüdischen Museum in der Oranienburger Straße 31 (Mitte). Neben solchen Kultgegenständen wurden vor allem Werke jüdischer Künstler ausgestellt. Viele Exponate sind seit der Plünderung von 1938 verschollen. (Bildarchiv Pisarek, Anfang 1933)

Old Berlin decorative Torah scroll covers and a circumcision chair from Märkisch-Friedland in the Jewish Museum at Oranienburger Strasse 31 (Mitte). Both these kinds of religious objects and works of Jewish artists were exhibited there. Many artifacts were permanently lost after the building was plundered in 1938. (Pisarek Photo Archive, early 1933)

Ansprache von Professor Franz Landsberger (1883–1964) zur Eröffnung des Jüdischen Museums am 24. Januar 1933, wenige Tage vor der nationalsozialistischen Machtübernahme. Landsberger war bis zu seiner Entlassung, die 1933 aufgrund des rassistischen »Gesetzes zur Wiederherstellung des Berufsbeamtentums« erfolgte, Ordinarius für Kunstgeschichte an der Universität Breslau und von 1935 bis 1938 Direktor des Jüdischen Museums. Nachdem er während des Novemberpogroms von 1938 im KZ Sachsenhausen interniert war, emigrierte er über England in die USA. (Abraham Pisarek)

Address held by Professor Franz Landsberger (1883–1964) at the opening of the Jewish Museum on January 24, 1933, just days before the National Socialists took power. Before he was laid off in 1933 as a consequence of the racist "Law for the Restoration of Professional Civil Service," Landsberger was a professor of art history at the University of Breslau. From 1935 to 1938 he served as director of the Jewish Museum. After being interned in the Sachsenhausen concentration camp during the November pogrom of 1938, he immigrated to United States. (Abraham Pisarek)

Die Innenansicht des Jüdischen Museums zeigt die rekonstruierte Einrichtung der Synagoge Schönfließ (Neumark) aus dem 18. Jahrhundert. Im Zentrum – typisch für orthodoxe Gottesdienste – befindet sich das erhöhte und umzäunte Vorlesepult und dahinter, zwischen den Fenstern, der Toraschrein. Das Museum wurde beim Pogrom 1938 verwüstet, geplündert und später geschlossen. (Bildarchiv Pisarek, Anfang 1933)

This view of the inside of the Jewish Museum at Oranienburger Strasse 31 shows the reconstructed synagogue room of the 18th century Synagogue Schönfliess (Neumark). Typical of orthodox prayer services, the raised and fenced in bima is located at the center with the Torah ark set between windows behind it. The museum was vandalized, plundered and closed down during the 1938 pogrom. (Pisarek Photo Archive, early 1933)

Schabbatfeier im Jüdischen Jugendwohn- und Lehrlingsheim Berlin-Pankow. Jeden Freitagabend wird zu Hause in der Familie mit Gästen oder – wie auf diesem Photo – zusammen im Heim ein festliches Schabbatmahl eingenommen. (Ca. 1931)

Sabbath celebration in the Jewish youth and apprentice home in Berlin-Pankow. In the Jewish tradition a ceremonial Sabbath dinner is prepared each Friday night at home with family and guests or as shown here in the youth home. (c. 1931)

Schachunterricht im Jüdischen Jugendwohn- und Lehrlingsheim Berlin-Pankow. (Ca. 1931)

Chess class in the Jewish youth and apprentice home in Berlin-Pankow. (c. 1931)

Moderne Rundfunktechnik wie beispielsweise diese Vielhöreranlage für Schwerhörige in der Synagoge Lützowstraße 16 (Tiergarten) wurde ganz selbstverständlich in liberalen Synagogen eingesetzt. (Abraham Pisarek, um 1930)

Modern technology like this multi-listening device for the hearing impaired at the synagogue at Lützowstrasse 16 (Tiergarten) was used without reservations in the liberal synagogues. (Abraham Pisarek, c. 1930)

כשר
Fleisch u. Wurstwaren
כשר
כשר
Oderbrucher
Fettgänse
כשר
כשר
Geflügel
27

Jüdischer Fleischerladen in der Linienstraße 27 (Mitte). Die hebräischen Buchstaben auf der mittleren Wandtafel lauten in der Übertragung: »Koschere Fleisch- und Wurstwaren unter streng ritueller Aufsicht des ostjüdischen Rabbinats«. Damit wurde vor allem eine aus Osteuropa stammende jüdische Kundschaft, der das Koscher-Zertifikat des Berliner Rabbinats nicht genügte, angesprochen. (1931)

Jewish butcher shop at Linienstrasse 27 (Mitte). The Hebrew text on the middle of the wall reads "Kosher meat and sausage under the strict ritual supervision of the Eastern Jewish rabbinate." This was directed foremost at the Eastern European Jewish customers who were not satisfied with the kosher certificate issued by the Berlin rabbinate. (1931)

Jüdische Buchhandlung und Leihbibliothek Rosenberg in der Grenadierstraße (heute Almstadtstraße, Mitte) im Scheunenviertel. Daneben werden auf einem Schild in hebräischen Buchstaben koschere Lebensmittel für Pessach angepriesen. Im Scheunenviertel existierten zahlreiche kleine jüdische Buchläden und Verlage sowie koschere Geschäfte, die die Bedürfnisse der hier lebenden orthodoxen Juden befriedigten. (Walter Gircke, 1928)

Rosenberg Jewish bookstore and library on Grenadierstrasse (today's Almstadtstrasse, Mitte) in the Scheunenviertel. The Hebrew sign next to it is advertising kosher food for Passover. In the Scheunenviertel there were countless numbers of small Jewish bookstores, publishers and kosher shops that catered mostly to the needs of the orthodox Jews who lived there. (Walter Gircke, 1928)

Purimfeier in der Schule der Jüdischen Reformgemeinde. Das Purimfest, das die Rettung vor der geplanten Vernichtung des jüdischen Volkes in Persien feiert, wurde Anfang der 1930er Jahre natürlich auf die aktuelle Bedrohung durch die Nationalsozialisten bezogen und spielte eine besondere Rolle in der Stärkung eines jüdischen Selbstbewusstseins. (Ca. 1933)

Purim celebration in the school of the Reform Congregation. In the early 1930s, Jews celebrating Purim, which recalls how the Jewish people were saved from extermination in Persia, made reference to the current threat posed by the National Socialists. The holiday was important in reinforcing the Jewish identity. (c. 1933)

Rabbiner Erwin Zimet (1912–1989) bei einer jüdischen Trauung. Zimet studierte in Berlin an der Universität und an der Hochschule für die Wissenschaft des Judentums. 1938 wurde Zimet als polnischer Staatsbürger im Rahmen der sog. Polenaktion mit seinem Vater nach Polen abgeschoben. 1939 gelang ihm mit Hilfe von Freunden die Emigration über England in die USA. (1933)

Rabbi Erwin Zimet (1912–1989) at a Jewish wedding. Zimet studied in Berlin at the university and at the Advanced School for the Science of Judaism. In late October 1938, as part of the so-called "Poland Action," Zimet and his father were deported as Polish citizens to Poland. Friends helped Zimet immigrate to the United States by way of England in 1939. (1933)

לא תנאף
לא תחמד

Abbildungen

Archiv für Kunst und Geschichte GmbH: 16, 17, 20, 21, 25, 34, 44, 45, 47, 50, 53, 54, 56, 57, 58, 59, 62, 63, 69, 70, 71, 80, 81, 82, 83, 85, 86, 88, 92, 98, 99, 100, 101, 103, 108, 114, 115, 118, 119, 120, 123
Bildarchiv Preußischer Kulturbesitz: 12, 14, 15, 18, 19, 22, 23, 24, 26, 30, 31, 32, 33, 38, 39, 40, 41, 43, 46, 51, 52, 55, 67, 68, 73, 89, 90, 91, 93, 94, 95, 96, 97, 104, 105, 109, 110, 124, 125
Jüdisches Museum Berlin: 5, 27, 28, 36, 37, 42, 49, 60, 64, 65, 66, 72, 74, 75, 76, 77, 78, 106, 107, 116, 117, 127
Leo Baeck Institute, New York: 13, 29, 35, 48, 61, 79, 84, 87, 102, 111, 112, 113, 121, 122, 126

Umschlag vorn: Mitglieder des Jüdischen Turnvereins Bar Kochba Berlin, 1902
Foto S. 5: Isi Kempler (geb. 1919), der Sohn von David und Liebe Kempler (vgl. S. 77) als Bar Mizwa mit Gebetsschal (»Tallit«). (W. Blutinger, 1932)
Umschlag hinten: Jüdische Buchhandlung und Leihbibliothek Rosenberg in der Grenadierstraße (Almstadtstraße). (Walter Gircke, 1928)